The
Charismatic
Gift of
TONGUES

The Charismatic Gift of TONGUES

Ronald E. Baxter

KREGEL PUBLICATIONS
Grand Rapids, Michigan 49501

Library of Congress Cataloging in Publication Data

Baxter, Ronald E., 1933-
 The Charismatic Gift of Tongues.

 Bibliography: p.
 1. Glossolalia—Controversial literature. I. Title.
BT122.5.B38   234'.13   81-17182
ISBN 0-8254-2225-6 (pbk.)   AACR2

Printed in the United States of America

CONTENTS

PREFACE

Without doubt *speaking with tongues* is the most prominent of the gifts claimed by the charismatic movement. It has commanded more attention and caused more division than any of the other mistaken claims made by neo-Pentecostalism. On every hand people are confused about tongues. Is this a gift of the Holy Spirit? Are tongues for today? What is their purpose? Are tongues the evidence of Spirit-baptism? If we say tongues have ceased, are we standing against the work of the Holy Spirit? Because of this uncertainty there is a great need for an indepth analysis of tongues. This work seeks to meet that need.

In doing so, let us remind ourselves that we must seek objective truth. What we determine must be upon the basis of God's Word and not subjective experience. We do not examine the Bible in the light of experience; but we do examine experience in the light of the Scriptures. Experience, and not the Bible, is the object to be verified.

Robert Lightner suggests that there are three evaluative criteria for facing the phenomenon of tongues:

> First, the criterion of judgment must be the Word of God and not the experience or experiences of man, either today or in past days. The real issue is not whether I am able to understand or explain the present claims, but what is the teaching of the Bible on the subject. Second, whatever is thought or said must be advocated with deep respect to the Holy Spirit. He is God the Holy Spirit and therefore sovereign. Third, it is not a matter of what He can or cannot do, but it is a matter of what He has chosen to do (57:17).

These are sensible evaluative criteria, and we shall seek carefully to follow them.

It is interesting to note also that our quest is not new. Indeed, it was the quest of those in Corinth, for what Paul wrote in 1 Corinthians chapters 12, 13 and 14 was at their request. Remember, Paul had preached at Corinth for almost two years before moving to Ephesus. Some feel that while there he had written a letter prior to 1 Corinthians, which is not a part of the Scriptures but in which he had given certain instructions to the church regarding order and holiness.[1] In turn, the Corinthian people had written some questions to Paul, and thus 1 Cor. 7:1, "Now concerning the things whereof ye wrote unto me" begins the answers to those questions.

It is in this light that chapter 12 opens, "Now concerning spiritual gifts, brethren, I would not have you ignorant" (1 Cor. 12:1). What Paul is presenting in this section are his answers to questions he had been asked. This causes Findlay to write:

> In treating of the questions of Church order discussed in this Div. of the Ep., the Ap.[2] penetrates from the outward and visible to that which is innermost and divinest in the Christian Society: (1) the question of the woman's veil, a matter of social decorum; (2) the observance of the Lord's Supper, a matter of Church communion; and now (3) the operation of the Spirit of God in the Church, wherein lies the very mystery of its life (16:884).

In this sense, Paul deals with the gift of tongues as a part of the total life of the body. He especially emphasizes understanding and order concerning this gift which had brought disorder (1 Cor. 12:33) and disrepute (1 Cor. 14:23) upon the church.

---

[1] G. G. Findlay gives a concise discussion of this in chapter 2 of the introduction to his *Exposition of 1 Corinthians*. He makes the point that references such as 1 Cor. 5:9-12 are to this earlier epistle. Paul may also have visited the Church at Corinth since leaving for Ephesus and that meeting may not have been very pleasant; hence, his reference in 1 Cor. 4:21 to *a rod* at his next visit (16:735 to 738).

[2] Findlay uses several abreviations in this passage. They are Div. (Division), Ep. (Epistle) and Ap. (Apostle).

With this introduction, let us examine the teaching of the Scriptures about tongues. It is our longing that, using this method, we shall be saved from the chaos, confusion and myths abroad in the movement which is the main exponent of this aspect of gift theology.

1

THE RECURRENCE OF TONGUES
IN THE BIBLE

In all, tongues are mentioned twenty-nine times in the New Testament. Of that number, twenty are found in 1 Corinthians chapters 12, 13 and 14. Speaking of these references, Scroggie writes:

It is quite a simple matter to classify these and the gain of doing so is immense, as the following facts show:
(1.) There is one reference only to *tongues* in the four Gospels.
(2.) There are three distinct references to tongues in the book of Acts.
(3.) There is reference made to tongues in only one of the twenty-one epistles of the New Testament.
(4.) There is no reference to tongues in the book of Revelation (58:6).

Surely these facts are significant enough to give us pause for reflection.

However, as we analyze the overall nature of the references to tongues in the New Testament, more startling information comes to light. As J. R. Boyd puts it:

1. The New Testament gives only two clear descriptions of the actual *use* of tongues. One of these is in Acts 2 and the other in 1 Corinthians 12-14.
2. The New Testament gives only one description of what actually took place when tongues were used (63:1).

The field of reference, upon which our doctrine concerning tongues is to be built, becomes obviously narrow.

It is time now to look separately at the five basic references to tongues given to us in the New Testament. First of all:

A. THE REFERENCE IN MARK 16:17

This reference to tongues is regarded as foundational to all others in the New Testament in that it is the ascension promise of Christ presented by Peter's young disciple, Mark.[1] The text says, "And these signs shall follow them that believe; In my name shall they cast out devils; they shall speak with new tongues." "Glōssais lalēsousin kainais"—"with tongues they shall speak new." This is the only reference to *tongues* in the Gospel narratives.

The word for tongue is *glōssa*, and for speak it is *laleo*. We shall look more closely at these when we begin to analyze Acts 2. Meanwhile it is sufficient for us to note that these are the regular words used for speaking with tongues in the New Testament.

But the expression *kainaia*, new, is different from all of the other occurrences. It refers to newness in the sense "of that which is unaccustomed or unused, not new in time." The newness is in "form or quality," making the object "of different nature from what is contrasted as old" (49:109).

Thus the "new tongues" of which Jesus spoke were not new in the sense that they had never been heard before. They were not "the tongues ... of angels" or some other "heavenly language" unlike those used or unused on earth, apart from those possessed of "the gift of tongues." Indeed they were not necessarily even new to the hearers, who may indeed fully understand what was being said.[2]

---

[1] While many reject the authenticity of Mark 16:9-20, believing it to be an interpolation, I am treating it as authentic. The subject of whether or not to accept the passage is outside the scope of this work. However, there are reasons for disagreement with the interpolation theory.

[2] Note Acts 2:8 where the statement of the polyglot crowd is based upon the fact that they understood what was being said in a language utterly familiar to them.

However, these tongues were to be "new" to the speakers, for they were to be different from those in which they were accustomed to speak. The implication is that the tongues would not be a learned language. "New tongues" would be a gift from God and would be a "sign"[3] to unbelievers of the reality of the new religion.

It is important to notice that Mark 16:17 merely mentions new tongues. There is no exposition of doctrine or description of their use. These both await further portions of the Word of God. We do not, therefore, build our doctrine for or against tongues-speaking solely on the statement of this text.

Further we need to note that Mark 16:20 tells us that the promises of verses 17 and 18 were fulfilled. There are clear implications in this fact which need to be noted and we shall do so later. Meanwhile, let us not, from Mark 16:17, say that because Christ promised new tongues they must necessarily be for today.

Let me illustrate. Suppose I promised you that I would come over and paint your house. Then suppose that after I did that (i.e. years later) you were to come to me and say, "You promised to paint my house. How about coming over and doing it now?" What would be wrong with your expectation? You would be forgetting that the promise made was already fulfilled years earlier. Thus does Mark 16:20 tell us that God kept His promises of verse 17 and 18—including that concerning "new tongues." Let us not, therefore, be mistaken and believe that He must fulfill His promise again.

This brings us to the first recorded passage in the Bible where the promise was fulfilled:

B. THE REFERENCE IN ACTS 2

This chapter describes the fulfillment of Christ's promise made some 10 days earlier (Acts 1:4-5). The facts are presented in historical narrative style, though the event was undeniably miraculous. Surrounding

---

[3] We shall deal with the word "sign" later. Sufficient for now is it to refer to 1 Cor. 14:22. See pages 41-54 for a full discussion on the implication of tongues as a sign gift.

events are described in language of analogy (i.e. sound "as of" a wind; tongues "like as of" fire). However, when stating the facts concerning the tongues-speaking, this analogous language disappears altogether. The statement is straightforward that they "began to speak with other tongues" (Acts 2:4).

Heterais glōssais (other tongues) is an important term. Glōssa can mean the tongue as the physical organ of the body. From there it comes to refer to the speech produced by that organ; thus, glōssa becomes a *language* (Acts 2:11). However, Acts 2:4 couples glōssa (language) with heterais (other), which makes a "generic distinction" (49:146). The language spoken was different from their native tongue but was still a human language. "The Greek word *heteros* would also indicate that the languages in which they spoke differed from one another in order that the men at Jerusalem, who had come from various lands, might understand the Gospel clearly" (56:7).

More than this, these heterais glōssais were *lalein* (spoken). "Laleō, to speak, is sometimes translated, to say" (49:323). What these disciples had to say, they spoke in languages other than their own. These foreign languages were the vehicles used by them to speak "the wonderful works of God" (Acts 1:11).

Luke's record concerning this event of Pentecost is even more exact as we come to verses 6 and 8. In these we are introduced to another word *dialektos,* meaning dialect.[4] Lewis Johnson says that:

> The word *dialektos* occurs about six times in Acts, and in each occurrence it refers to a known language or dialect. In other words, the sense of a known tongue in 2:4 is made definite by the description of the phenomenon as a speaking in dialektos in verses 6, 8 (71:309).

---

[4] It is unfortunate that neither in verse 6 nor 8 in the AV was the word *dialektō* translated by the more exact English equivalent *dialect.* In actuality one would not know from reading these texts that the same word is to be found in the original in both. The word *language* however, does come closer to the meaning than tongue.

The languages spoken on Pentecost are now described as particularized to the very dialect of the country or district from which the hearers came to Jerusalem.

This, of course, explains the amazement of Acts 2:7 and 12. These were uneducated peasants and fishermen who addressed them, yet they were able to speak in the dialect of these languages:

> Parthians, and Medes, and Elamites, and the dwellers in Mesopotamia, and in Judaea, and Cappadocia, in Pontus, and Asia, Phrygia, and Pamphylia, in Egypt, and in the parts of Libya about Cyrene, and stranger of Rome, Jews and proselytes, Cretes and Arabians (verses 9-11).

It would seem from verse 8 that the facility of language was so precise, that they spoke as though each dialect was their own, "in which (they) were born" (Acts 2:8). As Witty states:

> The point emphasized is that the crowd was amazed not by any strangeness of the speech or the actions but by the simple fact that they did understand. The entire record emphasizes understood speech, not meaningless sounds (52:43).

Therefore they could say, "we do hear them speak in our tongues the wonderful works of God" (Acts 2:11). They understood the language and could clearly identify the subject and respond to it!

This leads us to the jarring note of Acts 2:13. Some argue from this that the tongues were ecstatic utterances. However, note the distinction made here by the use of others, *heteroi.* This has the same root meaning of "other" *heterais,* applied to tongues in verse 4. It refers to a generic distinction. These mockers were *other* than the non-Palestinians mentioned previously. They were the Palestinian Jews whom Peter begins to address in verse 14. To them the other languages were a babble of unfamiliar sounds. Thus, the only conclusion they could find to explain the excitement and amazement produced upon these who did understand was that they were being disturbed by drunk men.

Notice also, before we leave Acts 2, that nowhere is mention made of *interpreters*. The fact is that those to whom "the wonderful works of God" were addressed needed no interpretation. They were hearing "every man in [his] own tongue, wherein [he] was born." The only ones who did not understand were the Palestinians themselves, "men of Judaea" and dwellers in Jerusalem (Acts 2:14). To them Peter began to explain the Biblical basis for the happening of Pentecost and to preach Christ crucified, risen and enthroned (Acts 2:14-36). The result was conviction of sin, repentance, faith in and obedience to Christ, and growth for the church (Acts 2:41).

Can Pentecost be duplicated today? Is the Charismatic Movement a return to Pentecost? Boyd says:

> To duplicate Pentecost, even in part, a group of Christians would need to go to a busy downtown street corner in Montreal, Toronto, New York or Los Angeles and miraculously start speaking seventeen of the languages represented in the neighborhood so that the people there would all hear the Gospel message in their own national tongues. This is never done, no matter how great the need or how many times the tongues-people are challenged to prove their claims by doing it. They simply cannot and do not repeat Pentecost even in this one, vital detail (63:7).

Don't be mistaken by neo-Pentecostal claims of a return to Acts chapter 2.

We come now to look at:

C. THE REFERENCE IN ACTS 10

In the earlier part of Acts 10, God had prepared Cornelius (Acts 10:3-6) and Peter (Acts 10:10-16) for the historic meeting in this Gentile's home. So great a break with tradition did this represent, that Peter addressed the group in the words of Acts 10:28, "Ye know how that it is an unlawful thing for a man that is a Jew to keep company, or come unto one of another nation; but God hath shewed me that I should not call any man common or unclean." The great lesson Peter had been taught was, "Of a truth I perceive that God is no respecter of persons: But in every nation he that feareth him, and worketh righteousness, is accepted with him" (Acts 10:34-35). This enabled him to associate with and preach to the Gentiles in Cornelius' home.

As Peter preached (i.e. "While he yet spake"—in the midst of his sermon!), an astounding thing happened in the eyes of the Jews, "The Holy Ghost fell on all them which heard the Word" (Acts 10:44). The Greek word used to describe their amazement at this is the same as that in Acts 2:12; they were "astonished" (Acts 10:45). The word has reference to the mind and applies to "that alteration of the normal condition by which a person is thrown into a state of surprise or fear" (47:52).

But what caused the amazement? What was the reason for it? It was, "because that on the Gentiles also was poured out the gift of the Holy Ghost. For they heard them speak with tongues, and magnify God" (Acts 10:45-46). They were astonished because, "The Holy Spirit never fell upon a Gentile" (22:262). Yet it happened and these Gentiles were *lalountō glōssais,* speaking with tongues. Surprisingly, Knowling comments on this tongues-speaking:

> ... here no speaking in different languages is meant, but none the less the gift which manifested itself in jubilant ecstatic praise was a gift of the Spirit, and the event may well be called "the Gentile Pentecost" (22:262).

Criswell also downplays the supernatural with the statement:

> Could it have been that in the household of the centurion there were soldiers, slaves, servants, and governmental officers from many of the nations of the Roman world? Could it have been that in their superlative, heavenly ecstasy they reverted each to his mother tongue in praising God for so great a salvation? It is a most commonplace psychological truth that in moments of extreme peril or delight a

foreigner will exclaim in his native language "in which he was born," rather than in the later language he has more recently acquired (10:209).

But what did actually happen? Two words tie the total happening to Pentecost; the word *also* in verse 45 and the word *for* in verse 46. The real reason for their amazement was that, as far as they could tell, what was happening was a near duplicate of Pentecost among the Gentiles. Later, when reporting to the apostles and the rest of the brethren in Jerusalem, Peter made this very clear:

> And as I began to speak, the Holy Ghost fell on them, as on us at the beginning.
> Then remembered I the word of the Lord, how that he said, John indeed baptized with water; but ye shall be baptized with the Holy Ghost.
> Forasmuch then as God gave them the like gift as he did unto us, who believed on the Lord Jesus Christ; what was I, that I could withstand God (Acts 11:15-17)?

He regarded the Spirit's bestowal upon the Gentiles in Caesarea to be as equally decisive as the bestowal upon himself and other Jews at Pentecost.

Notice that, as at Pentecost, there were no *interpreters* present. Apparently there was no need for them! The polyglot household of Cornelius would then correspond to the polyglot list of nationalities in Acts 2:9-11. We can assume that those who were listening understood what was said. Thus we read that, "They heard them speak with (languages), and magnify God" (Acts 10:46).

There can be no doubt about it, that the happening in Caesarea was as supernatural as that of Pentecost. The fact of the matter is that God did an unusual thing (i.e. "upon the Gentiles") in an unusal way. As Gardiner states:

> ... the outpouring at Cornelius' house followed Pentecost by eight years, yet Peter could not point to any continuous flow of such experience among the churches when he explained to the leaders at

Jerusalem what had happened to the Gentiles. After eight years he must say, "as on us at the beginning," not "as on all the churches." Here is a case where silence is eloquent indeed (17:9)!

Had Peter been able to point to the event as normative among the churches, surely he would not have reached back to Pentecost for confirmation of it.

But Pentecost was an historical event and not a continuing event, thus, it became the standard against which every other happening was judged. When the apostles and brethren heard the description of what happened, they completely concurred with Peter's handling of the matter, for we read, "When they heard these things, they held their peace, and glorified God, saying, Then hath God also to the Gentiles granted repentance unto life" (Acts 11:18).

In Acts 2 the Spirit fell upon the Jews and they spoke with tongues. In Acts 10 the Spirit fell upon the Gentiles and they spoke in tongues. Now we come to:

D. THE REFERENCE IN ACTS 19

In Acts 19:1-8 we have reference to a group of "disciples" who were neither Jewish nor Christian. Some charismatics have sought to prove from this passage that tongues were normative for that day and this. They have based their contention on the faulty Authorized translation of Acts 19:2 where we read the question, "Have ye received the Holy Ghost since ye believed?" As it stands, the text seems to state that the Spirit is received subsequent to salvation, as a kind of "second blessing." If this could be proven it would fit well with the charismatic doctrine of a baptism with the Spirit at a time later than conversion.

But what is Acts 19:2 really saying? The expression "since ye believed" is an aorist participle. A basic rule of Greek grammar requires the action of such a participle to be either simultaneous with, or antecedent to, the action of the main verb. In this case the main verb is "received." This means that the "receiving" must either precede belief, or be at one and the same time as belief.

"Since ye believed" is, therefore, an inaccurate translation, because it breaks the basic rule of grammar mentioned. For this reason, later versions translate Paul's question as, "Did you receive the Holy Spirit when you believed?" (83). The question was asked to determine whether they were saved, and not whether they had received a subsequent baptism of the Holy Spirit.

In this respect it fulfilled its purpose, for the answer was, "We have not so much as heard whether there be any Holy Ghost" (Acts 19:2). Under further examination it was discovered that they were followers of John the Baptist, still looking for the kingdom and Messiah to come. Not only had they not heard of the Holy Spirit, they had not heard of Christ. Thus, in verses 4 and 5 we have Paul's successful efforts to lead these people to faith and obedience in the Lord.

At this point we read, "And when Paul had laid his hands upon them, the Holy Ghost came on them; and they spake with tongues, and prophesied" (Acts 19:6). The word for tongues is the same as in Acts chapters 2 and 10. There is absolutely no reason to believe that the happening was any different from the other precedents, except that *languages* are tied to *prophecy* in this case. There was no interpretation involved and apparently was not needed. They were *languages,* which, though supernaturally given, were understood by others who heard them.

Far from bolstering the charismatic claim to some baptism of the Holy Spirit being evidenced by tongues and succeeding the day of conversion, this passage states the opposite: the day we are saved, that very day we receive the Holy Spirit. The fact of the matter is, if we have not received Him at conversion we have not truly believed, for, "if any man have not the Spirit of Christ, he is none of His" (Romans 8:9).

Another interesting fact emerges from an analysis of the three instances of tongues in Acts. In each case, *apostles were present.* Even on the occasion when the Holy Spirit was given but tongues were not mentioned (i.e. to the Samaritans in Acts 8:14-17), apostles were the vehicle for the happening. There is no instance in the New Testament of the laying on of hands for the receiving of the Holy Spirit apart from these apostles.

Can it be that this was solely an apostolic prerogative? It would seem so by the pattern developed in Acts. If this is the case, then there could not be a repeat of similar instances after the death of the apostles. Don't be misled, therefore, by those charismatics who would lay their hands on you so that you might receive the baptism of the Holy Spirit.

There is but one more recurrence of tongues mentioned in the Bible, that is:

E. THE REFERENCE IN
1 CORINTHIANS CHAPTERS 12, 13 AND 14

Speaking of the tongues claims by charismatics, J. R. Boyd states:

> Charismatics have a great variety of explanations and claims, some of which have no slightest scripture to back them up. Mostly though, they fall into two main classes of tongues as a sign and tongues as a gift. When they speak of tongues as a sign, they suggest that they relate to Pentecost. When they encourage tongues as a gift, then, of course, they relate to Corinthians (63:7).

But these distinctions are not only made among the neo-Pentecostalists. For example, Thayer defines the gift of tongues in 1 Corinthians as:

> the gift of men who, rapt in an ecstasy and no longer quite masters of their own reason and consciousness, pour forth their glowing spiritual emotions in strange utterances, rugged, dark, disconnected, quite unfitted to instruct or to influence the minds of others: Acts 10:46; 19:6; 1 Cor. 12:30; 13:1; 14:2, 4-6, 13, 18, 23, 27, 39 (43:118).

Others in an attempt to repudiate the modern tongues-movement have opted for a like interpretation.

It seems to me, therefore, that Walvoord is correct in issuing his warning that:

> Any view which denies that speaking in tongues used actual languages is difficult to harmonize with the Scriptural concept of a spiritual gift. By its nature, a spiritual gift had reality, and being supernatural, needs no naturalistic explanation (51:182).

When we come to Corinthians, there is no doubt that we are dealing with the gift mentioned in 1 Cor. 12:10,28 and 30.

These three chapters (1 Corinthians 12, 13, 14) hold some 20 references to tongues. In all of these the same vocabulary, as we have seen throughout Acts, is used. The word tongue is always glōssa and the word speak is always laleō. These are used in various grammatical forms but, nevertheless, all are identical in meaning to the three passages in Acts. "On the basis of the Greek and the statement of the text, no distinction can be found" (51:183).

Dillow calls our attention to the fact that Paul:

> ... specifically says that tongues are foreign languages spoken here on earth in 1 Cor. 14:10, 11: "Undoubtedly there are all sorts of languages in the world, yet none of them is without meaning. If then I do not grasp the meaning of what someone is saying, I am a foreigner to the speaker, and he is a foreigner to me. So it is with you." It is clear that the languages under discussion here in this chapter are those "in the world." Furthermore, the word translated *foreigner* is the Greek word barbaros, one who speaks a foreign language known here on earth.
>
> Paul's foregoing comparison between tongues and the sounds of inanimate musical instruments like harps and bugles (1 Cor. 14:7-10) merely implies that from whatever source they come, sounds must be distinct and meaningful. Paul is not suggesting that tongues are non-languages like musical sounds. Rather, the reverse, tongues must be distinctly spoken languages just as a note from a harp or trumpet must be distinct to be effective and meaningful.

In the face of this evidence, we have to conclude that New Testament tongues must have taken the form of meaningful, known words and languages (12:22).

Though the tongues spoken were other than the native language of the speakers, they were indeed *languages.* It was the way these languages were used, and not the languages themselves, that caused the outsiders to conclude that the speakers were mad (1 Cor. 14:23).

Paul's use of Old Testament reference in 1 Cor. 14:21 also argues for these being real languages. Certainly the reference in Isa. 28:11-12 must be taken to be real languages, indeed foreign languages.[5] Thus, the burden of proof again rests with modern charismatics to produce the like gift.

Don't be mistaken about the gift of tongues. There is a world of difference between the gibberish of today and the languages spoken in Bible times. Let the Bible be your infallible guide in your search for the meaning of *tongues,* then and now.

---

[5] We shall deal with this further when we come to discuss tongues as a sign gift. It shall then be abundantly clear that Paul's assumption is that the gift of tongues was a gift of speaking real *languages* to impress unbelieving Jews of God's impending judgment.

2

THE RELATION OF TONGUES TO SPIRIT-BAPTISM

In charismatic doctrine, the baptism in the Holy Spirit and the gift of tongues are invariably linked together. Several years ago the *Christian Herald* carried an article by Edward B. Fiske, religion editor for the *New York Times*. The article described Fiske's attendance at "a religious initiation rite"—obviously a charismatic group meeting—held "in the second floor music room of St. Edward's Roman Catholic Parochial School in Metairie, Louisiana, on the outskirts of New Orleans." Let this news reporter describe what happened in his own words:

> After about half an hour of instruction and informal worship, the standees placed their hands on the heads or shoulders of the initiates. Everyone closed their eyes and, after a brief silence, the room began to come alive with a crescendo of sound—exclamations such as "Praise Jesus!", long streams of seemingly random syllables, and appeals to the Holy Spirit to come upon each.
>
> Near the center of the room Mary Ann Willis, a 21-year-old handbag-and-hosiery saleswoman in a local specialty store, sat quietly for a short time. Then, seemingly without effort, she began talking in what seemed like a foreign language—"ye ked ee akay kan danee shangda." "The sounds just came out as if I had known how to do it my whole life," she recalled afterward. "It was so natural and beautiful. I felt great peace, inner peace and closeness of God. And I cried. You couldn't help but cry, it was so beautiful."

That evening marked Mary Ann Willis' "baptism in the Holy Spirit," and by it she joined the ranks of charismatic or neo-Pentecostal Christians who in the last few years have been rapidly increasing their numbers in Roman Catholic and several major Protestant churches (67:6).

Probably this description could be repeated a thousand times over, in a variety of communions, and always it would be the same. The "baptism" invariably produces, or is heralded by, tongues-speaking. Pentecostalist Donald Gee declares:

The distinctive doctrine of the Pentecostal churches is that speaking with tongues is the "initial evidence" of the baptism in the Holy Spirit. This article of belief is now incorporated in the official doctrinal schedules of practically all Pentecostal Denominations (18:17).

In his mind, therefore, the baptism with the Holy Spirit and tongues-speaking are inseparable.

What is "the baptism with the Holy Spirit?" When does it take place? Is it for everyone? What is its relationship to tongues? These and many other questions crowd our minds as we deal with the subject from a Biblical perspective. Therefore, that we might make an orderly analysis of the subject on hand:

A. LET'S CONFINE THE EVENT

One would think, by the major emphasis placed upon the baptism with the Holy Spirit today, that page after page in the New Testament deals with the subject. This is just not so. The baptism with the Holy Spirit is mentioned only seven specific times in the New Testament.[1] Of these:

1. FIVE PASSAGES POINT *AHEAD* TO PENTECOST

Each and every one of these has a common denominator; they are all connected with John's prophecy con-

---

[1] Though many believe that Rom. 6:3-4; Col. 2:12; Gal. 3:27; and Eph. 4:5 also refer to the baptism with the Holy Spirit, these can be interpreted equally well of water baptism.

cerning Christ. The first four of these references are
Matt. 3:11; Mark 1:8; Luke 3:16 and John 1:33. These are
the Gospel writers' basic record of John's statement. Let
the first suffice to illustrate the rest:

> I indeed baptize you with water unto repentance: but
> he that cometh after me is mightier than I, whose
> shoes I am not worthy to bear: he shall baptize you
> with the Holy Ghost, and with fire (Matt. 3:11).

The fifth of these also refers to John's prophecy about
Christ, except that in Acts 1:5 our Lord points to this as
being fulfilled in the promise referred to by Acts 1:4.
This is how Luke records the setting:

> And, being assembled together with them, com-
> manded them that they should not depart from Jeru-
> salem, but wait for the promise of the Father, which,
> saith he, ye have heard of me.
> For John truly baptized with water; but ye shall be
> baptized with the Holy Ghost not many days hence
> (Acts 1:4-5).

It is obvious that all five references, including this one,
are prophetic in nature. They are future in outlook,
anticipatory in concept and unfulfilled in time.

Beyond these portions:

2. TWO PASSAGES POINT *BACK* TO PENTECOST

These are Acts 11:15-17 and 1 Cor. 12:13. The first of
these refers to the falling of the Holy Spirit upon the
Gentiles in Caesarea. This event was astounding to the
Jews, to whom it never really occurred that Christ also
died for "the nations" outside of Judaism. Thus, when
Peter returned to Jerusalem to account for his unheard
of behavior in associating with (Acts 10:28), preaching to
(Acts 10:34-35), and baptizing of (Acts 10:47-48) these
Gentiles, he gave the following account as proof:

> And as I began to speak, the Holy Ghost fell on
> them, as on us at the beginning.
> Then remembered I the word of the Lord, how that
> he said, John indeed baptized with water; but ye

shall be baptized with the Holy Ghost.
Forasmuch then as God gave them the like gift as he
did unto us, who believed on the Lord Jesus Christ;
what was I, that I could withstand God (Acts
11:15-17)?

Peter's usage of the spirit-baptism prophetically
stated in the Gospels and Acts 1:5 to point back to Acts
chapter 2, clearly tells us that this was fulfilled at
Pentecost. Therefore what the Caesareans had done was
to show themselves participants in that historic event.
God had proven to the Jews that He intended the Gentiles to be full partners in the grace of God.[2] Such, of
course, is the emphasis of Ephesians 2:11-17.

Paul, also, points back in 1 Cor. 12:13. There he
recapitulates all other occurrences in one sentence, "For
by one Spirit are we all baptized into one body, whether
we be Jews or Gentiles, whether we be bond or free; and
have been all made to drink into one Spirit". *The American Standard Version* properly translates this text as,
"For IN one Spirit WERE WE all baptized into one
body."[3] *Ebaptisthēmen* "baptized", being the first
aorist passive indicative of *baptizō* "baptize", is a
reference to a definite past event (33:171).

This event is the same one to which the Gospel references looked forward. It is that which Jesus promised in
Acts 1:4-5 referring to John's prophecy. The same inci-
dent is recalled in Acts 11:15-16. All of these combined
refer to that historic happening on Pentecost, when the
baptism with the Holy Spirit was forever accomplished.

In saying this, several:

3. IMPORTANT FACTS MUST BE KEPT IN MIND

First, we must remember that the Gospel references
are statements of fact only. Doctrine is not discussed,

[2] Of the tongues of Pentecost, Witty says, "Similarly, the 'other' tongues
experience manifested, by the temporary breakdown of language barriers, the
new basis of human unity created by the pervading Spirit of Christ." (52:45)
"So the point to be emphasized here is the unity of all nations in the
brotherhood of Christ-redeemed man 'in the Spirit'." (52:46) It would seem
that the events in Caesarea formed a necessary lesson to emphasize this fact.

[3] Emphasis mine. This shows the corrected tense of the happening.

but an event is prophesied. All of them point away from John to Christ and are yet to be fulfilled.

Second, the Acts passages do not refer to doctrine but to fulfillment. They refer to the fact that John's prophecy would be fulfilled, and that it had been fulfilled. Thus, one passage (Acts 1:4-5) looks *forward* to Acts chapter 2 and the other (Acts 11:15-16) looks *back* to Pentecost.

Third, the Epistles are always our reference for doctrine. The Corinthian reference is, therefore, the interpreter of what was involved in the baptism with the Holy Spirit. It tells us that the Holy Spirit, as the active administrative agent of the Godhead carrying on the teaching and work of Christ in and through believers, was the element; and that the body of Christ was the sphere into which we were baptized.

This historic baptism took place at Pentecost. Both Acts 11:15-16 and 1 Cor. 12:13 tell us so. Therefore, Robert Wilson says, "Pentecost is unique, just as Calvary is unique. We have no more right to expect a recurrence of Pentecost than we have to expect a recurrence of Calvary" (79:5). The event is clearly confined in the Scripture and, forever after, the genesis of each believer's spiritual baptism is inseparably attached to that day, as surely as his salvation is tied to that other cataclysmic day when, "God the mighty maker died, for man the creature's sin."

Such an understanding of the event allows us to move another step forward. That we might form an orderly analysis of the baptism with the Holy Spirit:

B. LET'S DEFINE THE TERM

There are two ways in which we can attempt to define the baptism with the Holy Spirit: these are negatively and positively. Let us consider first:

1. WHAT THE BAPTISM WITH THE HOLY SPIRIT *IS NOT*

So much has been written in this subject that is non-Scriptural, confusing and wrong, that we need to define what the baptism with the Holy Spirit *is not,* before we can ever hope to understand what it is. Thus we can say that:

a. It is Not a Repeated Experience

1 Cor. 12:13 refers to a definite, historic event into which we all enter when coming into the body of Christ. We have seen that the construction of the term *baptized* refers back to that event. As A. J. Gordon put it:

> The upper room became the Spirit's baptistry, if we may use the figure. His presence "filled all the house where they were sitting," and "they were all filled with the Holy Ghost." The baptistry would never need to be re-filled, for Pentecost was once and for all, and the Spirit then came to abide in the church perpetually (19:56).

From that moment to this, the baptism with the Holy Spirit has been past tense and at conversion we are baptized into the body of Christ by being made partakers of that event.

Thus, the baptism is never repeated. The expression "were we" in 1 Cor. 12:13 tells us that it is past, it is all over. Each and every member of the body of Christ, therefore, has been baptized into "one body," in "one Spirit," by "one Lord," through "one faith," with "one baptism," by the grace of "one God and Father of all" (Eph. 4:4-5). The baptism with the Holy Spirit is not a repeated experience.

B. H. Carroll put it clearly when he told the story of a man who once asked him if he had received the baptism in the Holy Spirit. Carroll told him, "No, I didn't need it, for it was never given except to accredit the church, and I would be ashamed to say that 1,900 years had elapsed and Christ's Church was not attested."

Again we can say that:

b. It is Not a Subsequent Experience

Each believer is made partaker of the Spirit's baptism at *birth;* the moment our conversion places us in Christ and, thus in the body of Christ. It is interesting to note that in Acts 2:41 and 47 there are important omissions in the original. The word "them" and the expression "the church" are not found in these texts. The translators thought that by adding them in English the sense of the texts would be completed; but would not a better interpretation be, "unto the Lord?" This is clearly brought out in other verses such as Acts 5:14 and 11:24. At conversion men and women are made part of Him, placed in Christ and Spiritually baptized into His body.

Moule brings this out clearly when he states:

> The analogy of the Sacrament of Baptism would in itself lead us to connect the Baptism of the Spirit rather with the beginning of the new life than with a great development of it (29:222).

He goes on to speak of the happening on Pentecost and at Cornelius' house and says:

> Each may thus be held to typify and signify on a great scale the true birth-process and birth-time, by the same power, in the case of the individual soul (29:222).

He therefore believed that the baptism with the Holy Spirit was an entrance into our new life in Christ, and, therefore, occurred at conversion.

Again baptism with water marks the formal introduction of the believer into the church, the local manifestation of the body of Christ (1 Cor. 12:27). As surely as believers who have been scripturally baptized by immersion in the name of the Trinity into the visible membership of the local body of Christ (the church) are baptized once, so with Spirit-baptism. It occurs but once, and that at conversion, as the individual is spiritually joined to Christ and not on some subsequent occasion.

Then it is important to understand about the baptism that:

c. It is Not the Same As the Filling of the Holy Spirit

Because on the Day of Pentecost, as Acts 2:4 tells us, "they were all filled with the Holy Ghost, and began to speak with other tongues, as the Spirit gave them utterance," some have concluded that the baptism and the filling are the same thing. Indeed no less a Bible scholar than R. A. Torrey taught that the terms *baptism, filling and enduement* in relationship to the Spirit's work are interchangeable terms referring to the same thing (44:270). Thus he fell into the trap of saying that:

> The baptism with the Holy Spirit is an operation of the Holy Spirit distinct from and subsequent and additional to His regenerating work. A man may be regenerated by the Holy Spirit and still not be baptized with the Holy Spirit (44:271).

In saying that these terms are interchangeable, Torrey began applying the teaching of the New Testament regarding the filling of the Holy Spirit to the baptism.

Moody also was unclear on this matter. In his own life he seems to have interpreted the baptism as a second work of grace. In Moody's biography, after Torrey recounts the happening called his *baptism,* he comments:

> Once he had some teachers at Northfield—fine men, all of them, but they did not believe in a definite baptism with the Holy Ghost for the individual. They believed that every child of God was baptized with the Holy Ghost, and they did not believe in a special baptism with the Holy Ghost for the individual (45:55).

No wonder Ryrie states on this issue, "Confusion is compounded by the fact that great men like Torrey and Moody were unclear" (36:75).

However, the Scriptures make many differences between the filling and the baptism with the Holy Spirit. The following are representative:

First, there is no definite indication from the New Testament's verbal use of *Baptizo* "baptize", that continuous action is involved, but there is an indication of continuous action being involved in the New Testament's verbal use of *Plā-ra-ō* "filling".

Second, the baptism is not commanded, but the filling is. The venerable Handley Moule also states that:

> ... while the mentions of the holy filling are frequent, the recorded occasions of the Baptism are two only:

the Day of Pentecost, and the closely parallel occasion, when in the house of Cornelius, St. Peter, the
Apostle of Pentecost, was permitted solemnly and
forever to "open the door of faith to the Gentiles."
Nowhere in the Epistles does the precise phrase
"Baptism of the Spirit" occur. Are we not thus led to
the conclusion that the Baptism is not to be identified with the filling, and is not, like the filling,
presented to us as a blessing for which the Christian
is to seek (29:221).

He is right. Any fair reading of the Word of God leads to
this same conclusion.

Nowhere in the Gospels, Acts, Corinthians—or in any
other portion of the Scriptures—are we told to seek the
baptism, or to pray and tarry for it. But in Eph. 5:18
plerousthe "filled" is in the imperative mood, the mood
of command, leaving no doubt that God intends for us to
seek the filling of the Holy Spirit.

Third, the baptism is positional but the filling is
experimental. Since the baptism with the Holy Spirit in
the Scriptures is an historic event in which we all had a
part, it is, in a very primary sense, positional in nature.
It is positional as having our names in "the Book of
Life" in heaven is positional (Phil. 4:3), or as "sitting
together in heavenly places in Christ Jesus" is positional
(Eph. 2:6). The baptism is that which God does in
establishing our relationship with Christ and the fellow
members of His body. On the other hand, the filling is
the experimental inflow of Divine power. It, therefore,
radically affects the way we live, how we witness, and
what we do for Christ. The outflow of that filling is the
experiencing of Eph. 5:19-21 in one's daily life.

For these and other reasons, we can clearly see that
the baptism with the Holy Spirit is not the same thing as
the filling with the Spirit.

We can say further concerning the Spirit-baptism presented in the Scriptures, that:

d. *It is Not for a Select Group of Believers Only*

One characteristic of the modern tongues-movement is
that of spiritual pride. The impression often given is,

"I've got it and you haven't. I'm sorry for you!" But 1 Cor. 12:13 makes it abundantly clear that "all" have been baptized who have been saved. There was not a person in the Corinthian membership who was not baptized with the Holy Spirit (1 Cor. 12:13), though all did not speak with tongues (1 Cor. 12:30).

Furthermore, this coincides with Peter's statement concerning the promised baptism (recorded in the Gospels and Acts 1:4-5) on the day of Pentecost. "For the promise is unto you, and to your children, and to all that are afar off, even as many as the Lord our God shall call" (Acts 2:39). The promised baptism fulfilled on Pentecost is the automatic gift of the Spirit to the believing heart at conversion.

Of the baptism with the Holy Spirit, it can further be said that:

e. It is Not an Answer to Agonizing Prayer

Many talk of "tarrying" for the baptism. They quote fervently Christ's instructions to His disciples in Luke 24:49, "And, behold, I send the promise of my Father upon you: but tarry ye in the city of Jerusalem, until ye be endued with power from on high." Thus, agonizing and emotional prayer, sometimes of great length, is entered into. Tarrying meetings are set up and young Christians are instructed in how to receive the baptism.

However, this verse, as with the instruction of Acts 1:4-5, was for the disciples in pre-Pentecost days. Written over those days was the explanation of John 7:39, "The Holy Ghost was not yet given." These instructions were specifically for the disciples (Acts 1:13-15) during the ten days between the ascension of Christ and the descending of the promised Spirit.

The story is told of a man who came to Dr. Harry Ironside one night and said, "I have just come from a great tarrying meeting. Hundreds have been tarrying for many days in San Jose, California, waiting for the Holy Ghost." Ironside asked by what authority they were doing this. "Why Jesus said, tarry ye in the City of Jerusalem, until ye be endued with power from on high." To this Ironside replied with quick wit and straight theology, "Well, my friend, are you not confounding the location and time? You are over 10,000 miles too far away, and over 1,900 years too late."

Well said! Tarrying was for Jerusalem for 10 days prior to Pentecost, A.D. 33. Nowhere in the Bible are we taught to pray, or seek for the baptism with the Holy Spirit. Absolutely nowhere! All believers are baptized with the Spirit, or they are not joined to Christ.

Though it has been said elsewhere, let us emphasize it again concerning the baptism with the Holy Spirit:

f. It is Not Any Evidence of Spirituality

Keep it well in mind that 1 Cor. 12:13 was written to the Church at Corinth (1 Cor. 12:27). This was, however, manifestly the most unspiritual church of all those to whom Paul wrote. The sixteen chapters of 1 Corinthians entirely unmask their character. They were sectarian (1-2), carnal (3-4), immoral (5), unloving (6), marriage breakers (7), unseparated (8-10), despisers of the Lord's Table (11), undisciplined in worship (12, 13, 14) and untaught in the Scriptures (15-16).

Yet, with all of this, they were Christians who were washed, sanctified and justified (1 Cor. 6:11). And more, they were baptized with the Holy Spirit (1 Cor. 12:13). Further, they came "behind in no gift" (1 Cor. 1:7). You see, the baptism and the gifts—even tongues—are not a sign of spirituality or of personal growth. They are the gifts of God's grace (charis), bestowed at conversion upon people as undeserving of them as they are of salvation.

Having defined the term negatively, we are now ready to define it in positive terms which tell us:

2. WHAT THE BAPTISM WITH THE HOLY SPIRIT *IS*

Inasmuch as the word is used but seven times in the New Testament in the unique sense of the Spirit's work, and inasmuch as six of these are quoting John's prophecy, one can see that there is a real danger at this point to yield to the temptation to "fill in the gaps" with subjective fancies. This, of course, is exactly the charismatic problem. Many are pontificating teaching which is just not in the Bible.

Now having said that, there are a number of things which the Holy Spirit has seen fit to explain in God's Word, with regard to the *what* of spiritual baptism. First of all:

a. It is Baptism in the Element of the Holy Spirit

Note again 1 Cor. 12:13:

> For by one Spirit are we all baptized into one body, whether we be Jews or Gentiles, whether we be bond or free; and have been all made to drink into one Spirit.

The preposition *en* (by in the AV) is best taken in a locative sense[4] in the original, referring to the element in which the person is baptized. Hence, a better preposition in translation would be "in". Findlay states that "in" "defines the element and ruling influence of the baptism (into) the relationship to which it introduces" (16:890).

The physical counterpart of water baptism well illustrates the point. A person in becoming a part of the local body of Christ is immersed in the sphere of water. The water thereby becomes the element in which the baptism takes place.

Just so at Pentecost the Holy Spirit "filled all the house where they were sitting" (Acts 2:2). They were immersed in His presence. Thus was fulfilled the historic baptism of which John had spoken. So also, at conversion we are made partakers in that historic immersion. This happens in the same way in which we are made partakers of Calvary in salvation. As Lehman Strauss observes:

> The use of the word *baptism* usually marks an initial experience. It is so when one is regenerated. Im-

---

[4] However, whether we accept the preposition as locative, or by the instrumental as many do, makes little difference to our interpretation. As Unger says: "This is Spirit baptism whether the Greek preposition 'en' is construed as the instrumental 'by' or the locative of sphere 'in'. To show the precise meaning in Greek of the phrase 'Spirit baptism', we can express it in English as in-the-sphere-of-the-Spirit baptism." (46:137)

mediately upon accepting the Lord Jesus Christ as personal Savior, a newly-saved sinner is baptized into the Body of Christ. He need never seek the baptism as a "second work of grace", for such teaching is not derived from the New Testament (41:151).

Secondly, we can say that:

b. It is the Work of Jesus Christ

In our illustration of physical baptism, we have seen that the water is the sphere in which the candidate is immersed; but that leaves the need for a baptizer. Obviously the element is not the baptizer, neither is the church to which he is joined by baptism (except as the baptizer is under the authority of that church). So in spiritual baptism. The element is the Holy Spirit, but who is the Baptizer?

In each of the references to John's prophecy in the Gospels, it is evident that the baptism is to be performed by our Lord. There is no doubt, also, that when Jesus referred to John's statement in Acts 1:5 He tied it to Himself by the words of verse 4, "Wait for the promise of the Father, which, saith He, ye have heard of me." Always, while the Spirit is seen to proceed from the Father He is sent by our Lord, or in the name of our Lord (John 14:26; 15:26; 16:7).

Strauss is clear on the historical aspect of this matter when he writes:

> The baptism with (or in) the Spirit is always the work of the Lord Jesus Christ. He alone is the Baptizer. We never read of anyone being baptized by the Spirit. Of a truth every believer has been baptized by our Lord in the Spirit. When we are saved, we become a vital part of the already-baptized body of Jesus Christ. The baptism took place at Pentecost, and it is the first operation that is applied to the believing heart (41:150).

Thus the baptism with the Holy Spirit, whether we are referring to Pentecost or to the application of Pentecost to the newly regenerated soul at conversion, is the work of Christ Himself.

Now this is important for our interpretation of 1 Cor. 12:13. You see, while the Holy Spirit is the element in which the believer is baptized, there is no reference to the One performing the baptism. Thus we bring to bear, in our interpretation of this text, all that has been gleaned from the previous references—namely those tied to John's prophecy. When we do so, we are left with the obvious conclusion that Christ Himself is the Baptizer.[5]

A third point concerning the *what* of Spirit-baptism is that:

c. It is Fundamentally Tied to the Local Church

What body was that of which Paul spoke when he said, "For by one Spirit are we all baptized into one body, whether we be Jews or Gentiles, whether we be bond or free; and have been all made to drink into one Spirit" (1 Cor. 12:13)? He goes to great lengths to illustrate what he means by reference to a physical body in verses 14 to 26. What body does he illustrate?

Fortunately, we are not left to speculate. Outrightly, Paul tells this Corinthian Church to which he writes (1 Cor. 1:2), "Now ye are the body of Christ, and members in particular" (1 Cor. 12:27). Can anything be clearer? The baptism with the Holy Spirit spoken of in verse 12 is tied to a local church as the physical manifestation of Christ's body.

There were "many members" in that local church and each one was *particular* because of his gifts, but *all* were there by the Spirit's baptism. Their membership was the result of their baptism with the Holy Spirit. The water-baptism which related them physically to that local body was only valid upon the basis of the Spirit-baptism already experienced.

This has a clear message for those in the charismatic movement who downplay "organized religion" and re-

---

[5] It is freely granted that the work of Christ on earth is accomplished by the Holy Spirit, but He does so as the representative of Christ. Thus Christ is the Baptizer by the work of the Spirit in the heart of the newly regenerated soul. However, in this work one is made a partaker in the historic baptism on Pentecost, which is clearly and only the work of Christ.

fuse to identify with the local church. Fundamental to Spirit-baptism is membership in a local "body of Christ". To emphasize the baptism while at the same time downgrading membership in a local church is a contradiction in terms.

A person, therefore, who receives Christ, yet frowns upon the local church, its ordinances, and its membership, is clearly putting himself out of step with the Biblical teaching on the baptism with the Holy Spirit. The charismatic Prayer Groups where Spirit baptism is sought and dispensed, by-passing the authority of the local church and the teaching of the Word of God, clearly are as out of step with Biblical reality as was the ministry of the "seven sons of Sceva" (Acts 19:13-17). Don't be misled by such legendary charismatic definitions of doctrine.

This background enables us to move now to a more specific discussion of the baptism as it relates to tongues. In doing so:

C. LET'S DECLINE THE MYTH

What is the Pentecostal and charismatic myth with regard to the baptism with the Holy Spirit? It is that when one receives the baptism he will speak in tongues. This is the evidence — initial or otherwise — of Spirit-baptism, as taught in these twin movements.

Let us be clear at the very outset that the baptism with the Holy Spirit is not the basis for the gifts of the Spirit. I have in my study several books by charismatic preachers. The following are some samples of their position on this matter. Emil Solbrekken, a Canadian exponent writes:

> As it was in Bible times, so it is today; the sign of speaking with tongues *always* accompanied the baptism of the Holy Ghost. When you, my Christian friend, *receive* the Holy Spirit, you too will *speak with tongues and magnify God,* just like Mary, the mother of Jesus, Peter, James, John and the other early Christians. If you haven't spoken with tongues, how can you say you have received what they re-

ceived. Has God or His Word changed? If you *want what they had,* you have to receive it the way God gives it — *God's way* (59:17)!

Speaking with tongues is the initial, outward *sign* that a believer has received the Baptism of the Holy Ghost (59:19).

Stephen B. Clark, a Roman Catholic writer states:

Normally when a person is baptized in the Spirit he has a definite experience. Commonly this experience is connected with the gift of tongues. This experience is important for him in being able to live the life of the Spirit (53:20).

Oral Roberts explains:

It is a baptism, a coming upon, a filling and a gift. These terms are synonymous when applied to receiving the fullness of the Holy Ghost. The book of Acts clearly points out that speaking in tongues was a practice of those who received the fullness of the Holy Spirit (32:18).

You will notice that this last quote from probably the most famous living charismatic makes the same mistake Torrey made in confounding several terms. Out of this flows his doctrine and when he speaks of "the filling of the Holy Spirit" he refers to the baptism with the Holy Spirit also.

But no matter, not once in all the Bible is it taught that the baptism is the basis for receiving the gifts of the Holy Spirit in general and the gift of tongues in particular. If it were, then, when one received the baptism he would, as our charismatic friends proclaim, receive the gift of tongues. But, patently false is this seen to be when one reads 1 Cor. 12:28-31. The gifts were sovereignly given and not everyone was an apostle, or a prophet, nor did all speak with tongues!

The fact is that a careful study of the first half of the chapter indicates that the gifts were a bestowal apart from the baptism with the Spirit. The baptism is tied to our placement in the body and to that alone. At the time of conversion a number of things happen to us, including the receiving of our personal gifts, but this must not be confounded with the work of Spirit-baptism.

Apart from 1 Corinthians 12, the other main passage which gives a base to the gifts of the Holy Spirit is Mark 16:17-18.[6] In this passage the gifts are tied solely to belief in the Lord Jesus Christ for the salvation mentioned in verse 16. Even though John's promise of baptism is recorded in Mark 1:8, there is no attempt to connect this to the gifts at the end of the Gospel, though a simple repetition of the earlier passage would have done so. Apparently Mark connected the gifts uniquely to one's conversion, giving the basis for their reception as faith in Jesus Christ as Savior and Lord.

Writing shortly after the turn of the century, W. Graham Scroggie faced the claims of the Pentecostal movement in its early days. It drove him back to the Word of God to see "whether those things were so" (Acts 17:11). Then he wrote:

> To speak with tongues is something for which large numbers of Christians are desirous, and even praying. This is not to be wondered at, if these utterances are really the sign of the Spirit-baptism. But as they are not, serious doctrinal error lies at the bottom of such a desire and expectation. Moreover, Scripture nowhere exhorts us to desire this gift; indeed, its exhortations move in the opposite direction (58:33).

Oh, that many more with clear heads and warm hearts would arise in our generation to follow in his train.

For some the search after the baptism with the Holy Spirit is an emotional catharsis. Witness this account by a Presbyterian woman:

> All the joys of my life were blended together in one ecstatic moment—all the fun of childhood, my first date, the moment when the man I wanted asked me

---

[6] Acts 2:1-4, which is often claimed as a base for the charismatic teaching on Spirit-baptism, is a description of the coming of the Holy Spirit in answer to Christ's promise. It is not a statement of foundation for the baptism with the Holy Spirit. The fact is that unless one deliberately confounds the terms baptism and filling, Spirit-baptism in not mentioned.

to share life with him, the exultation of the finished
sex longing ... I had the sensation I was almost
floating instead of walking (65:13).

For others it is emotional masochism. This is well illustrated in the following recollection by J. R. Boyd:

I knew a fine, big German Christian in Sudbury
named Bill Kripps, years ago, who was saved in Pentecostal meetings in Pembroke, but who never suc-
ceeded in getting what he called "The baptism", at
least as long as I knew him, even though he tarried,
prayed and begged in their meetings many times. He
also tortured himself with self-abusing searchings to
discover the secret of unconfessed sin that kept the
Spirit out. I was convinced that Bill was a better and
more honest Christian than most of those were who
abused him with the charges that said he must have
secret sins or he would get the Holy Spirit and speak
with "tongues" (63:3).

With telling candor Donald Gee, himself a Pentecostalist, supplies more of the answer than he realizes, in
saying:

Some baptisms are disappointing because some
people have been urged to speak in what seem to be
tongues, and I doubt if they have really had the baptism at all (18:28).

The problem, of course, with Gee's statement is that he
does not go far enough, for tongues-speaking in totality
has nothing to do with the baptism with the Holy Spirit.
Therefore, whatever the emotion produced, whatever the
effect seen, there is absolutely no relationship between
tongues and the Bible doctrine of Spirit-baptism. Don't
be mistaken by the experience minus reality in truth.

3

THE REGULATION OF TONGUES
IN CORINTH

While in 1 Corinthians chapters 12, 13 and 14 some 13 of the spiritual gifts are mentioned, the majority of teaching centers on the gift of tongues. It is evident that this gift had been causing problems in the assembly and when they had written to Paul for teaching on a variety of concerns, the matter of tongues-speaking had been among them. Thus, chapter 14 in its entirety is given over to the regulation of tongues in the church.

This interpretation of Paul's purpose is stated by W. A. Criswell in these words:

> The discussion of Paul is not a list of exhortations to speak in tongues, but a long enumeration of restrictions against the practice. The Apostle is not encouraging the Corinthians to exercise the gift but to refrain from its use. He is not presenting a set of rules to glorify the congregation in tongue-speaking, but he is rather laying down stringent regulations to restrain this thing that has broken out in the church. Paul is hedging the gift on every side (10:212).

It is important for us to realize this fact in determining what is really being said in the chapter.

What regulations do we find set forth in this Scripture regarding the gift of tongues? First of all, the whole thrust of the passage teaches us that:

A. TONGUES ARE TO BE RECOGNIZED AS INFERIOR

This point was clearly emphasized in the two lists of chapter 12; in both, tongues and interpretation are listed last. Especially is this significant when we discover that in the second list (1 Cor. 12:28) Paul deliberately underscores a Biblical order of importance.

> And God hath set some in the church, first apostles, secondarily prophets, thirdly teachers, after that miracles, then gifts of healing, helps, governments, diversities of tongues.

Notice the way he does this, using numerical identification of the first three, followed by the expressions "after that" and "then." By the time he gets to "diversities of tongues," it is obvious that he is implying these to be the least of the gifts.

The same theme recurs in chapter 14 where he states in verse 5:

> I would that ye all spake with tongues, but rather than ye prophesied: for greater is he that prophesieth than he that speaketh with tongues, except he interpret, that the church may receive edifying.

Later in verse 19 he adds, "Yet in the church I had rather speak five words with my understanding, that by my voice I might teach others also, than ten thousand words in an unknown tongue" (1 Cor. 14:19). Paul is exalting the gifts that actually communicate the Gospel truth. Thus, he exhorts them to "utter words easy to be understood" (1 Cor. 14:9).

There can be absolutely no doubt about it, in Paul's mind, tongues were the least of the gifts. The mistake being made in the Corinthian assembly was to emphasize the gift which was minor to the rest. His regulations, therefore, have the effect of rectifying this matter by getting their attention back on the most significant gifts.

The second regulation unveiled is that:

B. TONGUES SHOULD BE USED TO EDIFY

Edification, in Paul's mind, is the primary principle of worship. If what is done does not build up the spiritual lives of those present, then the exercise is a failure. So it is with tongues.

> Now, brethren, if I come unto you speaking with
> tongues, what shall I profit you, except I shall speak
> to you either by revelation, or by knowledge, or by
> prophesying, or by doctrine (1 Cor. 14:6)?

This principle of edification is not a subjective one. To
build up oneself by "private" use of tongues, merely
feeds the ego. Hence 1 Cor. 14:4 makes the contrast, "He
that speaketh in an unknown tongue edifieth himself;
but he that prophesieth edifieth the church." The irony
is clear—selfishness edifies self; selflessness edifies
others. Therefore he continues, "Even so ye, forasmuch
as ye are zealous of spiritual gifts, seek that ye may excel
to the edifying of the church" (1 Cor. 14:12). If tongues
do not edify others, then they ought not to be used.

The third regulation tells us that:

C. TONGUES MUST BE INTERPRETED

Paul's argument on this point is particularly
devastating. Notice these statements from 1 Cor. 14:5:

> I would that ye all spake with tongues, but rather
> that ye prophesied: for greater is he that prophesieth
> than he that speaketh with tongues, except he inter-
> pret, that the church may receive edifying.

Do you see how Paul regards the matter of tongues in
relation to interpretation? He wants them to be able to
speak in tongues, but only if they themselves can interpret. Only then will tongues have profit for the entire
assembly.

Verse 6 emphasizes this fact also:

> Now, brethren, if I come unto you speaking with
> tongues, what shall I profit you, except I shall speak
> to you either by revelation, or by knowledge, or by
> prophesying, or by doctrine?

Only languages that he can translate for them will be of
use to the church as he communicates a "revelation,"
speaks a word of "knowledge," makes a prophetic utterance, or explains some "doctrine."

After enlarging on the need for clear utterance of our communication to the church (verses 7-12) the apostle writes his coup de grâce on the matter. Note the following, "Wherefore let him that speaketh in an unknown tongue pray that he may interpret" (1Cor. 14:13). Do you see that in this verse he effectively neutralizes tongues in the church? What is the sense of speaking a matter twice — once in an unknown language, and once in an interpretation — when a single delivery in simple, understandable speech will do? Anyone who has attended a dual-language church service, where translation of the sermon was necessary, will realize that it takes twice as long to say half as much! Furthermore, by the time the language of one's understanding is taken up again the impact of the previous sentence can be largely lost.

By implication, this is Paul's message as he calls for the tongues-speakers to neutralize their own gifts. Eventually one would be bound to say, "Why give the foreign language portion at all? I may as well simply give the interpretation to begin with, so that the people may understand and be edified." Such a modified use of tongues would automatically elevate the gift to the stature of prophecy and, hence, Paul's reason for "except he interpret" in verse 5.

In the fourth place they were regulated in that:

D. Tongues Must Warn Unbelieving Jews

We shall deal with this in detail in the next chapter, however, it is important for us to note that Paul quotes from Isa. 28:11-12. In doing so he calls tongues, "a sign, not to them that believe, but to them that believe not" (1 Cor. 14:22). What does this mean?

Paul has just finished admonishing the Corinthians about their childish admiration for tongues. He is now explaining to them that, rather than being an exhilarating emotion, tongues had a very serious purpose. Indeed they have a punitive character, he tells them in verse 21. Says Findlay:

According to the true interpretation of Isa. 28:9ff. (see Cheyne, Delitzsch, or Dillmann ad loc.), the drunken Israelites are mocking in their cups the teaching of God through His prophet, as though it were only fit for an infant school; in anger therefore He threatens to give His lessons through the lips of foreign conquerors (11), in whose speech the despisers of the mild, plain teaching of His servants (12) shall painfully spell out their ruin. The *hōti* "for" is part of the citation: "For in men of alien tongue and in lips of aliens I will speak to this people; and not even thus will they hearken to me, saith the Lord". God spoke to Israel through the strange Assyrian tongue in retribution, not to confirm their faith but to consummate their unbelief. The Glossolalia may serve a similar melancholy purpose in the Church (16:909).

These tongues were, therefore, neither to instruct the church, nor to convert the world. They were the judicial *sign* of God's judgment about to fall on Israel.

Because this was so, the occasions for their use were limited. Only when unbelieving Jews were present were tongues to find the fulfillment of their purpose. All other settings where the Corinthians were using them had no Scriptural sanction upon them. Tongues were, therefore, regulated by their function of being a sign of warning to unbelieving Jews.

The fifth regulation tells us that:

E. TONGUES ARE TO BE PLANNED

It is often a surprise to those involved in the charismatic movement to learn that tongues-speaking in the Bible was not necessarily spontaneous. In this the miraculous gift of tongues differed greatly from the uncontrolled ecstatic states of the Greek mystery religions. Paul alludes to this in 1 Cor. 12:2, "Ye know that ye were Gentiles, carried away unto these dumb idols, even as ye were led". It is a picture of worshippers out of control, "carried away" in emotional hysteria.

But the gift of tongues, bestowed by the sovereign work of the Holy Spirit, was not to be uncontrolled. Rather the totality of the worship services where they were used were to be planned and orderly. Paul's admonition was, "Let all things be done decently and in order (1 Cor. 14:40). Thus, should anyone insist that God was leading him to speak, he must wait his turn. Only one was to speak at a time and only a maximum of three were to speak altogether (1 Cor. 14:27).

Furthermore, before a person could speak in tongues he had to make sure that an interpreter was present. The rule was emphatic, "If there be no interpreter, let him keep silence in the church" (1 Cor. 14:28). There were to be no "off the cuff" utterances in the hope that someone might be able to translate. Rather, there was to be enough prior planning to determine that an interpreter for the given tongue was present.

This clearly means that the same was true of tongues as was true of prophecy.

> And the spirits of the prophets are subject to the prophets.
> For God is not the author of confusion, but of peace, as in all churches of the saints (1 Cor. 14:32-33).

Tongues were never to generate confusion, were never to be out of control, but were always to be orderly, planned and God glorifying. The application of such an emphasis today would remove much that deprecates the name of Christ because of the unscriptural and injurious practices of today's Charismatic Movement.

Regulation number six was explosive!

F. Tongues were Forbidden to Women

In 1 Cor. 14:34 and 35 the church is addressed with regard to their women prophesying or speaking with tongues. There we read:

> Let your women keep silence in the churches: for it is not permitted unto them to speak; but they are commanded to be under obedience, as also saith the law. And if they will learn any thing, let them ask their husbands at home: for it is a shame for women to speak in the church.

Without doubt, women were forbidden to speak in tongues by this Scripture.

Now why would this be? Several reasons could be given:

1. GOD'S CHAIN OF COMMAND

The totality of Scripture indicates a chain of command under God (1 Cor. 11: 3, 8-9). Paul states this simply in 1 Cor. 11:3:

> But I would have you know, that the head of every man is Christ; and the head of the woman is the man; and the head of Christ is God.

Women are not to usurp authority in the local church (1 Tim. 2:12). They are also to be under the authority of their own husbands at home (Eph. 5:22-23). The answer as to why Paul forbade women to speak in tongues may therefore be found in this Biblical theology.

2. THE HEATHEN BACKDROP

The answer may also have been found in the heathen backdrop of ecstatic utterance and temple prostitution so evident in Corinth.

The city was famous for its immorality, much of which was vented under the guise of religion in the temple of Aphrodite.[1] There temple prostitutes engaged in ritualized sexual orgies, often whipping themselves up into ecstatic frenzies. In the midst of these orgies, these frenetic women would utter ecstatic "tongues" in dedication to heathen gods.

Paul's abhorance of this would be very understandable. He would not want the heathen in Corinth to identify the church in any way with the tragic scenes of pagan temple worship. Thus, to make the line of difference as clear as possible, women were forbidden to speak in tongues or to prophesy.

[1] F. F. Bruce states, "For many centuries Corinth enjoyed great commercial and naval prosperity. Its reputation, as might be expected in a great seaport, was none too good on the moral side. Indeed, the Greeks had a verb to denote indulgence in the more abandoned forms of wantonness—korinthiazesthai, they called it, 'behaving as they do in Corinth.'" (5:3). Part of that behavior was garbed in religion.

Note clearly the strength of language Paul uses in this, "It is a shame for women to speak in the church" (1 Cor. 14:35). The word shame refers to something "base, shameful, opposed to modesty, or purity" (50:16). The indictment is strong and has never been removed from the Word of God. It is, therefore, of as much authority today as it was when Paul wrote it.

3. THE SIGN WAS FOR UNBELIEVING JEWS

There is a further thought as to why Paul may have written this interdiction: the sign was to "unbelieving Jews".

To the Jews, women were on the same plane as slaves, or dogs. To hear a woman speak in tongues would not only be repugnant to the Jews but would also defeat the purpose of the sign gift.

Whatever the reason, be it these or some other from the counsels of God's inscrutible plan for mankind, women were forever forbidden to speak in tongues. Should the modern neo-Pentecostals adhere to this Biblical regulation the Charismatic Movement would collapse overnight.

There is one last regulation mentioned by Paul:

G. TONGUES WERE NOT TO BE FORBIDDEN

In 1 Cor. 14:39 Paul wrote, "Wherefore, brethren, covet to prophesy, and forbid not to speak with tongues." Much appeal is made to this text by today's charismatics. To them it is proof positive that no one should dare to state that they ought not to be practicing tongues today. But this overlooks one minor detail. In the day Paul immediately addressed, tongues were still needed and practiced. The day of their demise had not yet come, thus, anyone who would forbid to speak in tongues would be forbidding the Spirit of God to have expression through His chosen vessel.

However, if the Word of God teaches that the Biblical purpose for tongues has been fulfilled, and that tongues have ceased; then the matter is seen in a different light. Not only should we forbid tongues as an un-Biblical aberration but as an extra-Biblical phenomenon. Far from being opposed to the teaching of Scripture, therefore, we would be upholding the unique message of the Word of God, which was attested to and finalized during the signatory period of miracles and wonders and signs in the first century.

Well writes James W. Bryant:

> Those in the modern tongues-movement justify the disruptiveness their practices cause in churches by accusing those who resist the movement of being unspiritual. Paul jumped the gun on them. He said, "If any man think himself to be spiritual, let him acknowledge that the things that I write unto you are the commandments of the Lord" (1 Cor. 14:37). A truly spiritual person will apply the Word of God to the tongues phenomenon today and come up with the right answers. God is not going to let his church dissolve itself in disruption, nor perish in the chaos of confusion. He will bring us through this crisis. He will enable us to discern the true gifts of the Spirit from that which is counterfeit. He will give to our hearts a spiritual acknowledgement of the truth of God's Word (7:77).

Don't be mistaken about the temporary nature of tongues and their regulation in the New Testament.

4

THE REASON FOR TONGUES
WAS A SIGN

Always and in all places our appeal and standard for belief and practice must be the Word of God. If the Bible is contrary to our beliefs and practices, then it must not be the Scriptures which are discarded but those things which are not according to the Word of God. To put it another way with regard to the subject on hand, the appeal of a real Christian is not to experience but to the Scriptures.

Jesus said, "Search the Scriptures" (John 5:39). Paul wrote, "Study to show thyself approved unto God, a workman that needeth not to be ashamed, rightly dividing the Word of Truth" (2 Tim. 2:15). Of the Berean believers Luke recorded, "These were more noble than those in Thessalonica, in that they received the Word with all readiness of mind, and searched the Scriptures daily, whether those things were so" (Acts 17:11). At all times and in all circumstances our appeal must be to the Word of God.

Nowhere is this more important than when we deal with the reason for speaking with tongues. No experience, however wonderful or uplifting, can ever be allowed to supersede the teaching of the Word of God. So, with Isaiah of old we say, "To the law and to the testimony: if they speak not according to this word, it is because there is no light in them" (Isa. 8:20). If what we learn from the Scriptures cuts across our experience, then we ought to call a moratorium upon our practice; until we search the Scriptures and come to grips with God's Word, even if that destroys our system of experiential theology.

Unfortunately, not many people are willing to study the Scriptures to discover such an important fact as the purpose for tongues. Perhaps this is the reason for today's charismatic confusion. In order to be clear on this matter, let us now seek from the Scriptures what is the Bible reason for tongues.

In doing so, we discover that:

A. THE GIFT OF TONGUES HAS AN OLD TESTAMENT BASE

In 1 Cor. 14:20-22 we read:

> Brethren, be not children in understanding; howbeit in malice be ye children, but in understanding be men.
>
> In the law it is written, With men of other tongues and other lips will I speak unto this people; and yet for all that will they not hear me, saith the Lord.
>
> Wherefore tongues are for *a sign*, not to them that believe, but to them that believe not: but prophesying serveth not for them that believe not, but for them which believe.

This is the one and only God-given, direct and specific reason for the gift of tongues that we find in the Bible.

For this reason Paul reaches back into the Old Testament. He quotes from Isa. 28:11-12 where we read:

> For with stammering lips and another tongue will he speak to this people.
>
> To whom he said, This is the rest wherewith ye may cause the weary to rest; and this is the refreshing: yet they would not hear.

Thus, to understand the Old Testament base for tongues, we must seek to discover what Isaiah is saying.

The content of Isa. 28 is set in the latter years of King Hezekiah of Judah who reigned from 705-701 B.C. Before his rule, in the year 722 B.C., Assyria had invaded Palestine and the Northern Kingdom, Ephraim, had been destroyed. Now, some 17 years later, Isaiah is warning the people of the Southern Kingdom, Judah, that the same thing is going to happen to them.

You see, instead of trusting in the Lord for deliverance from Assyria, Judah has made an alliance with Egypt. This has brought a fresh influx of heathen practice amongst God's people, and their hearts are turning from the Lord. In Isaiah 28:7-8 Isaiah has come upon a case in point, the leaders of Judah in a drunken party. Thus we read:

> But they also have erred through wine, and through strong drink are out of the way; the priest and the prophet have erred through strong drink, they are swallowed up of wine, they are out of the way through strong drink; they err in vision, they stumble in judgment. For all tables are full of vomit and filthiness, so that there is no place clean.

The leaders of Judah have degenerated into drunkards who wallow in the filth of their own vomit.

But the leaders refuse Isaiah's assessment of Judah's spiritual standing. Indeed, they sneer at the prophet, calling his doctrine simple and childish. They do not appreciate being spoken to as though they were children. Their question is:

> Whom shall he teach knowledge? and whom shall he make to understand doctrine? them that are weaned from milk, and drawn from the breasts.
> For precept must be upon precept, precept upon precept; line upon line, line upon line; here a little, and there a little (Isa. 28:9-10).

As far as they are concerned, Isaiah is an intolerable moralist and they would be free adults and not hampered children. Yet they are being taught like infants instead of grown ups by this overbearing prophet and they sneer at his warnings.

Isaiah now begins to deal with them at the very point of their sarcasm. In verses 11-13 he makes a prophetic announcement of coming judgment. Since the people would not listen when God speaks to them in plain and simple Hebrew (their native tongue), He will now speak to them in a language they cannot understand, in Assyrian. Thus we read:

> For with stammering lips and another tongue will he speak to his people.
> To whom he said, This is the rest wherewith ye may cause the weary to rest; and this is the refreshing: yet they would not hear (Isa. 28:11-12).

These new tongues, heard upon the streets of Jerusalem and throughout the land, would herald God's judgment upon them. The tongues would be the sign which would point them directly to Isaiah's warning and prophecy of coming judgment.

Now the thought of God's people being addressed by foreign tongues was a common judgment theme in the Old Testament. We find it in Deut. 28:15-68, which records Moses' prophecy of judgment through the invasion of Palestine in A.D. 70. In verse 49, Moses states part of that judgment as:

> The Lord shall bring a nation against thee from far, from the end of the earth, as swift as the eagle flieth; a nation whose tongue thou shalt not understand.

Note that this part of the coming judgment meant being subjected to a language that they could not understand.

All through the Old Testament to be addressed in foreign tongues in their own homeland meant God's judgment upon the Jews. In this light, Isa. 28:11-12 was warning of impending judgment. The "stammering lips and another tongue" was God's judicial sign of judgment upon them, because they hardened their hearts against the simple truths His prophet had spoken.

It is in this light that we must understand Paul's statement that tongues are a sign. In Isaiah's day God summoned Assyria to be His instrument of judgment. The sign of the Assyrian language in the streets and throughout the countryside heralded the fulfillment of Isaiah's prophecy.

But in Paul's day the Jews are again an apostate nation. They have rejected their Messiah. Now once again the sign of tongues appears and, to Jews familiar with the Old Testament Scriptures, this meant only one thing — judgment.

We can readily see now, that:

B. THIS OLD TESTAMENT PROPHETIC BASE GIVES THE PURPOSE FOR TONGUES IN THE NEW TESTAMENT

Interestingly enough, before Paul refers back to Isaiah, he prefaces his quote with a caution against *childishness.* "Brethren, be not children in understanding: howbeit in malice be ye children, but in understanding be men" (1 Cor. 14:20). It would seem more than chance that this statement precedes his appeal to Isa. 28:11-12, in view of the background to the verses Paul is quoting. There, childishness was very much the issue. Here, Paul warns against immaturity in relation to tongues — "Do not continue the childish attitude of your ancestors in Isa. 28:9 and 10!" He also is warning them not to overlook the purpose for which God gave the gift of tongues, as they overlooked the statement of judgment in relation to tongues made by Isaiah.

Then follows the Old Testament quotation of 1 Cor. 14:21, "In the law it is written, With men of other tongues and other lips will I speak unto this people; and yet for all that will they not hear me, saith the Lord." As surely as Isaiah's purpose statement for "other tongues" was that of judgment, just as surely Paul's deliberate conclusion is that the New Testament tongues were also a sign—not of salvation, but of judgment. Robertson and Plummer also interpret the passage in this light:

Tongues have a further use, as a sign to unbelievers, not a convincing, saving sign, but a judicial sign. Just as the disobedient Jews, who refused to listen to the clear and intelligible message which God frequently sent to them through His prophets, were chastised, by being made to listen to the unintelligible language of a foreign invader, so those who now fail to believe the Gospel are chastised by hearing wonderful sound, which they cannot understand. If this is correct, we may compare Christ's use of parables to veil His meaning from those who could not or would not receive it (34:316).

This is brought out very clearly in the apostle's use of the Greek word *hōste,* rendered wherefore in the Authorized Version. What is to follow is plainly the result of a legitimate deduction from the Scriptures just presented. So we read, "Wherefore tongues are for a sign, not to them that believe, but to them that believe not: but prophesying serveth not for them that believe not, but for them which believe" (1 Cor. 14:22). In the orginal the phrase *eis sēmeion* "for a sign", involves a frequent Greek idiom which expresses purpose. It indicates (together with hōste) that the apostle has discovered the true intent of the Old Testament phenomenon just quoted.

To make this even more specific, there is a definite article attached to tongues in the original. It is *ai glōssai* "the tongues" which are *eis sēmeion* "for a sign". This confirms that Paul regards the New Testament gift of tongues to be the particular phenomemon meant by the Old Testament prophecy just quoted. In other words, it was not simply tongues in general to which Isaiah of old refers but to "the tongues" of which these three chapters of 1 Corinthians speak.

Paul is therefore particularizing the Old Testament passage quoted to the Jewish nation. In its original setting the expression "this people" can refer to no other people. Isaiah is, therefore, said to have foretold the rejection of Messiah's ministry and words by the nation Israel. Thus the true function of tongues is to be "for a sign ... to them that believe not."

The expression in the original is "eis sēmeion ... tois apistois." In our English translation, the adjectival construction of *tois apistois* "them that believe not" is not distinguished from the preceding participial construction *tois pisteuousin* "them that believe" but they are not identical. Zane Hodges explains that:

> The fact that either two participial constructions, or two adjectival ones, could have been used if precise, exact opposition of the two expressions were intended points to the conclusion that a certain shade of difference existed in the apostle's mind. (Footnote

states: Direct opposition could be achieved by tois pisteuousin and tois apistousin, or possibly more likely, tois pistois and tois apistois. The adjective apistos occurs again in verses 23 and 24 as a description of basic character). The adjective apistos under these circumstances would—in contrast to a participial form—express pure description as over against the action of believing involved in the foregoing participle. Thus apistos, as a description, is more static and hence more inherent in tone. Accordingly, even this grammatical nicety seems emphatic with the spirit of the Isaiah prophecy which deplores a condition of unbelief so tragically fixed that not even the sign-gift of tongues can arouse the nation from it (70:230).

It is clear, therefore, that what Paul is saying in 1 Cor. 14:22 arises specifically from the Scripture quoted in verse 21 and is judicial in nature.

What was the New Testament purpose for signs, then? It was to speak to "this people" (i.e. Jews) about their unbelief and the impending judgment it was about to bring upon the nation. Only in this light does verse 23 make sense, since, if the gift of tongues is truly a sign to the generality of "them that believe not," then any time an unbeliever is present would be an appropriate time to exercise the gift. Paul, however, clearly states in verse 23 that the opposite is true, because, to the heathen, speaking in tongues was a sign of madness and not of judgment!

We are ready now to discover that:

C. THE NEW TESTAMENT PURPOSE FOR TONGUES
IS SEEN IN THE BOOK OF ACTS

Since the book of Acts is the history book of the New Testament, we should expect to see Paul's stated purpose for tongues illustrated in life situations. There are only three occasions on which tongues are seen in the entire book.[1] Can we see in these occurrences the confirmation of tongues as a sign to unbelieving Jews concerning impending judgment?

Let us first of all:

1. LOOK AT ACTS CHAPTER 2

In this passage it is clearly evident that unbelieving Jews were present. Apart from the generic list of languages represented by Acts 2:9 to 11, Peter's sermon makes it abundantly clear that many others were present. These were all "Jews, devout men, " but they were responsible before God for rejecting their Messiah.

In fact, the charge of murdering the Messiah is set forth bluntly in verse 23, where it is said to the people concerning their treatment of Jesus, "Ye have taken, and by wicked hands have crucified and slain." Then verse 36 proclaims, "Therefore let all the house of Israel know assuredly, that God hath made that same Jesus, whom ye have crucified, both Lord and Christ" (Acts 2:36). Here, Peter is asserting that Israel is now under the judgment of God for their part in crucifying the Messiah. This called for repentance and faith in Jesus as Savior and Lord.

Now the proof that what he was saying was correct had been the tongues of verse 4. The sermon Peter preached began with an explanation of tongues and went on to state why the nation was, as proven by these "other tongues," under judgment. Thus, the tongues of Acts 2 were a sign upon which Peter built his sermon and which produced the cry of verse 37 and response of verse 41. In this way Paul's statement of 1 Cor. 14:21-22 was illustrated on Pentecost.

The second illustration is found when we:

2. LOOK AT ACTS CHAPTER 10

Some will seek to deny the authenticity of our interpretation by stating that Acts 10 deals with Gentiles only.

---

[1] Some interpret Acts 8 as also being an occasion when tongues were spoken. This view holds that when Acts 8:18 says that Simon "saw (i.e. by way of some outward manifestation) that through laying on of the apostles' hands, the Holy Ghost was given," it means that the sign gift of tongues was the evidence of the reception of the Holy Spirit.

This is only partially true. To state the fact that Peter was a virtual unbeliever as far as the grace of God extending to the Gentiles is concerned is not at all an overstatement. The vision of Acts 10:11 to 15 was repeated three times (v.16) because Peter would argue (v. 14) with God about the meaning of the vision. After the third time, we read that, "Peter doubted in himself what this vision which he had seen should mean" (v. 17).

Furthermore, even after the brave statements of verses 28 and 34-35 were uttered, it is evident that Peter and his companions "were astonished, as many as came with Peter, because that on the Gentiles also was poured out the gift of the Holy Ghost. For they heard them speak with tongues, and magnify God" (Acts 10:45-46). They were virtual unbelievers that Israel was no longer the exclusive people through whom God would work but that the Gentiles were on an equal basis with Jewish converts.[2] These tongues, therefore, gave a final chilling ring to the message of judgment upon Israel, whose rejection of the Messiah had now become the salvation of the Gentiles.

This thought is emphasized in Acts 11:2-3 for "when Peter was come up to Jerusalem, they that were of the circumcision contended with him, Saying, Thou wentest in to men uncircumcised, and didst eat with them." These Jews just did not believe that Israel's favored nation status was set aside and that Gentiles were now elevated to be partakers of "the covenants of promise." It was only when Peter could recount:

> And as I began to speak, the Holy Ghost fell on them, as on us at the beginning.
> Then remembered I the word of the Lord, how that he said, John indeed baptized with water; but ye shall be baptized with the Holy Ghost.
> Forasmuch then as God gave them the like gift as he did unto us, who believed on the Lord Jesus Christ; what was I, that I could withstand God? (Acts 11:15-17).

[2] Compare Acts 11:19 where we read that it never occurred to those people that God was interested in saving any but "the Jews only." So it seems to be with Peter and his companions in Acts 10 until vs. 46.

—only then, when the sign of tongues was evident, do we read "When they heard these things, they held their peace, and glorified God, saying, Then hath God also to the Gentiles granted repentance unto life" (Acts 11:18). MacArthur puts it:

> The message to Israel was clear. No longer would God confine Himself to one people as a channel; no longer would God operate His work of grace through one nation and speak one language. Their unbelief changed that. Tongues, then, were the sign of the removal of national blessing on Israel (24:168).

To learn that the Gentiles were at the center of God's plan, for the new age, was to learn that Israel was not; but, that as a nation, they were under impending judgment. Thus once again the point made by Paul in 1 Cor. 14:21-22 was corroborated in an actual life situation.

But there is a third laboratory in which to test this interpretation.

3. LOOK AT ACTS CHAPTER 19

Here we are faced with a group of Jews who were influenced by the ministry of John the Baptist. He was long gone, but this group of loyal disciples, with limited knowledge were seeking to live up to the light they had. However they did not know Christ as Messiah and Savior, neither therefore, had they received the gift of the Holy Spirit.

As the Gospel of Christ was preached, they believed and were baptized. But, as was the case in Samaria,[3] they apparently did not receive the gift of the Holy Ghost, until Paul laid his hands upon them in apostolic prerogative. So, "when Paul had laid his hands upon them, the Holy Ghost came on them; and they spake with tongues, and prophesied" (Acts 19:6).

---

[3] In the case of the Samaritans, though they were saved and baptized (Acts 8:12), the Holy Ghost had as yet "fallen upon none of them" (Acts 8:16). It was not until Peter and John exercised the apostolic prerogative of laying on of hands in this connection that, "they received the Holy Ghost" (Acts 8:17).

Now two things are important here. Apparently, judging from verses 8 and 9, there were many Jews in Ephesus and many of them unbelieving. The fact that these 12 men "spake with tongues" was a fulfillment in their ears of Isaiah's prophecy of old, freshly quoted by Paul in 1 Cor. 14:21. Judaism was slated for judgement!

The second thing to be noted is that what happened in Ephesus fundamentally connected the work of God there with the work of God in Jerusalem. These disciples were hundreds of miles away from "the holy city," the center of God's dealings with the Jews, therefore, what happened in Ephesus served as a sign to Israel that God's program no longer centered in Israel. God's purpose would now be worked out worldwide without reference to Jerusalem, the Messianic capital. Again it was being underscored that the casting away of Israel in God's judgment was underway, as Isa. 28:11-12 had stated it would be.

Thus, we discover that each of the three historical occurrences of tongues in Acts happened in accordance with Paul's statement of 1 Cor. 14:21-22. Jews were involved in each occurrence and judgment can be seen to be the underlying thread of unity. There can be no doubt that the gift of tongues was a sign to unbelieving Jews about impending judgment in fulfillment of Isa. 28:11-12.

This brings us back to Paul's purpose statement:

D. THE TEACHING OF CORINTHIANS IS TO RE-EMPHASIZE THIS PROPHETIC PURPOSE FOR TONGUES

The declaration of 1 Cor. 14:22 is clear, "Wherefore tongues are for a sign, not to them that believe, but to them that believe not." Apparently these Corinthian believers had forgotten this—if they had ever known it. Hence, Paul re-emphasizes the fact in bringing sanity to the situation in the church regarding this spiritual gift.

Remember that Corinth was a world city. It was international in character and had a thriving Jewish community.[4] Paul had ministered there sometime previously (Acts 18:1-18), at first mainly to the Jews (Acts 18:5) but later "when they opposed themselves, and blasphemed, he shook his raiment, and said unto them, 'Your blood be upon your own heads; I am clean; from henceforth I will go unto the Gentiles'" (Acts 18:6). Thus at Corinth there was a society of not only unbelieving but also of intolerant and bigoted Jews (Act 18:12-17).

Tongues, therefore, could play a very vital part in speaking to these people. There was every opportunity of fulfilling Isaiah's prophecy in their ears. The judicial warning it held would have had great relevance amongst them, for bear in mind that tongues was a sign of impending judgment upon the unbelieving nation.[5] As Findlay says:

> Through an alien voice the Lord speaks to those refusing to hear, by way of "sign to the unbelieving" (1 Cor. 14:22). These abnormal utterances neither instruct the church nor convert the world (16:909).

They were merely God's judicial sign of judgment upon unbelieving Israel.

By the way, the reason for interpreters in the church was for the Gentiles, not the Jews. If the "tongues" at Corinth corresponded to those at Pentecost, Caesarea and Ephesus (which we have every linguistic and interpretive reason to believe, as we have already seen), then the Jews understood them, [6] for they were primarily addressed to them. But the Gentiles, not understanding these languages, were in danger of entering the church and concluding, because of the unintelligible speech they heard, that the people were "mad" (1 Cor. 14:23). Thus,

[4] Some of these Jews were there because they had been expelled from other places in anti-semitic purges (Acts 18:2). At Corinth they found an international mosaic that enabled them to settle down and make a permanent home. Others were there because it was a thriving business center and they regarded their stay as a short term business venture (James 4:13-17).

[5] See Findlay, G. G., "St. Paul's First Epistle to the Corinthians," *The Expositor's Greek Testament.* 5 Vols. Grand Rapids, Michigan: Wm. B. Eerdmans Publishing Com. 1956, Vol. II, pages 909-910.

[6] See Acts 2:6,11; 10:46; and Acts 19:6 where "tongues" are tied to "prophecy," the latter being given understandably in the former.

in the church the supernatural ability to address the gathering in a foreign tongue was not to be exercised unless an interpreter was present to translate to those Gentiles who did not understand the language.[7] In this way the primary function of tongues could be fulfilled, without bringing unwarranted disrepute upon the church.

Now when Paul wrote 1 Corinthians, the church was already forgetting the original purpose of tongues and, therefore, it was a priority to re-emphasize this prophetic reason. If it was important for Paul to do so in the first century, when as yet the command, "Forbid not to speak with tongues" (1 Cor. 14:39) had current validity, surely it is doubly important to do so today. The purpose of tongues was to signal God's judgment on Israel.

In Luke 21:20-24 Christ gave to Isaiah's prophecy a more current application.

> And when ye shall see Jerusalem compassed with armies, then know that the desolation thereof is nigh. Then let them which are in Judaea flee to the mountains; and let them which are in the midst of it depart out; and let not them that are in the countries enter thereinto.
> For these be the days of vengeance, that all things which are written may be fulfilled.
> But woe unto them that are with child, and to them that give suck, in those days! For there shall be great distress in the land, and wrath upon this people.

[7]This may be a good time to interject that some hold the miracle of Pentecost to be in the speech of the speakers and others in the ears of the hearers. Philip Schaff explains the event as both a miracle of speech and hearing in these words:

> The foreign spectators, at least a number of them, believed that the unlettered Galileans spoke intelligibly in the different dialects represented on the occasion. We must therefore suppose either that the speakers themselves were endowed ... with the gift of foreign languages not learned by them before, or that the Holy Spirit who distributed the tongues acted also as the interpreter of the tongues, and applied the utterances of the speakers to the susceptible among the hearers (52:44).

It is obvious that at Corinth, if this was the case with the Jews, it certainly was not so with the Gentiles who needed an interpreter.

> And they shall fall by the edge of the sword, and
> shall be led away captive into all nations: and Jeru-
> salem shall be trodden down of the Gentiles, until the
> times of the Gentiles be fulfilled.

As has been said constantly, the tongues of Pentecost,
Caesarea, Ephesus and Corinth heralded such judgment.

But did it happen or do we yet wait for it to take place?
Yes, it happened very literally in A.D. 70 when the invading armies of Titus swooped down upon the city of
Jerusalem. Inexplicably, Titus pulled away from the ex-
tended siege for a short while and the believers,
remembering Christ's prophecy, fled the city and were
saved. The unbelievers were slaughtered or taken
prisoner and the city was literally demolished. In order
to get the gold which had melted in the ensuing fire and
which had run down between the stones of the Temple
walls, the very stones of that magnificent structure were
pried apart by the invaders and left in a heap (Matt.
24:1-2).

Thus did Isaiah's prophecy meet its Messianic fulfillment. Hence also did the purpose for "the tongues"
come to an end. There was no longer a need for a judicial
sign of judgment. It had already happened. The age-long
treading down of Jerusalem constitutes a visual lesson
to our world, as long as it continues, that God's purposes
with the Jews as a nation are in abeyance and His purposes for the Gentiles are predominant. Thus, the purpose for the gift of tongues is gone. Don't be misled,
therefore, by those who say that the sign is for today.

5

THE REMOVAL OF TONGUES
BY MATURITY

Our thesis for this chapter is that tongues have ceased. Here lies the dividing line between the charismatic and the historic fundamental, orthodox position. If Biblical tongues have indeed ceased, then the neo-Pentecostal position is wrong and should be shunned by all Bible-believing Christians.

The question arises immediately, "How do we determine whether tongues have ceased or not?" There are two methods proposed, one Biblical and one non-Biblical. Some say we can know:

A. BY EXPERIENCE

This is basically the position of the Charismatic Movement. "You cannot deny my experience," say these people. This is a feeble argument. Most cults coming to our door, or meeting us on the street, or trying to sell us literature can also talk about their *experience.* Does this mean that we should embrace their doctrine?

One does not build the house of his Christian life upon the shifting sands of experience but upon the impregnable rock of the Holy Scriptures. Experience is not the interpreter of the Bible; the Bible is the interpreter of experience. The judge of experience is the Bible; experience is not the judge of the Bible.

Gerry Benn puts the point well in writing:

> I am not obligated to validate or invalidate anyone's experience. I want to know what God has to say in His Word regarding these phenomena. Instead of subjectively trying to discover if something is

legitimate, I want to objectively look at the claims of the charismatics based on the only absolute standard of measurement, the living Word of God (62:2).

Experience is not a firm foundation upon which to build one's life and practice.

Much is made by charismatics of John 9:25 where we read the testimony of the blind man who had been healed by Jesus to be, "one thing I know, that, whereas I was blind, now I see." They say, "There you are, experience is a valid basis for belief." But wait a moment. What is the real story of John 9? Is it not primarily a lesson to Christ's disciples (verses 1-5)? And did not the man's experience have its foundation upon the Word and work of Christ? The Word of Christ stated, "I am the light of the world" (John 9:5). The work of Christ is expressed in verse 6, "When he had thus spoken, he spat on the ground, and made clay of the spittle, and he anointed the eyes of the blind man with clay." Now, on the basis of the Word and work of our Lord, the man was obedient to Christ's command, "Go, wash in the pool of Siloam, (which is by interpretation, sent)" (John 9:7a). Finally we read the result, "He went his way therefore, and washed, and came seeing" (John 9:7b).

The man had an experience alright, but it could be validated upon his obedient response to the Word and work of Christ. What he says in verse 25 is merely the answer deserved by those who rejected both the words and works of our Lord (compare John 9:4 with John 10:26-27; and 9:24 with 15:24). Thus, even in John chapter 9 the message is clear that experience is not the standard, but rather the inerrant and unchanging Word of God is.

This brings us to the second method for determining whether tongues have ceased:

B. By Scripture

The Psalmist said, "For ever, O Lord, thy Word is settled in heaven" (Psalm 119:89), but that Word has been delivered to us here upon earth. Therefore, he continues, "Thy Word is a lamp unto my feet, and a light unto my path" (Psalm 119:105). The Word of God now becomes the infallible guide to the very course of our lives. To the Psalmist, the only sure method for determining belief and practice was that unchanging word, forever settled in the heavens.

Isaiah clearly lays out the alternatives for us in chapter 8 verses 19 and 20. Verse 19 is well representative of experience not founded upon the Word of God.

> And when they shall say unto you, seek unto them that have familiar spirits, and unto wizards that peep, and that mutter: should not a people seek unto their God? for the living to the dead?

No one could deny that weird things happened around these people. Even Isaiah does not deny the experience, but he does deny that it is according to the Word of God. Thus, he gives us the inerrant measure for determining truth, "To the law and to the testimony: if they speak not according to this word, it is because there is no light in them" (Isa. 8:20). God's unchanging standard of truth is the Bible alone.

In this chapter we seek to determine what the Bible declares with regard to the cessation of tongues. By doing so we shall find that 1 Cor. 13:8 gives us a direct statement regarding this matter, and that 1 Cor. 13:9-12 gives us a full explanation as to why. The first interpretative need we have in this is:

1. A WORD STUDY

This allows us to determine the subject matter about which we speak. Notice that in 1 Cor. 13:8 there are three basic gifts in view. First of all there is:

a. Prophecy

The verb is *prophēteuō,* meaning simply "to forthtell." As a noun *prophētēs* refers to one who has insight into divine things and who speaks them forth to others. A prophecy, then, was an authoritative revelation from God concerning the present and the future. It was a message of special revelation for the local church to instruct and edify.

The prophetic gift differed fundamentally from the teaching gift. In the teaching gift, there is no more revelation or authority than the Scriptures upon which it is based. However, the prophetic gift had its authority in the direct reception of divine truth, which in turn was communicated verbally, or (as in the case of the Bible) in written form.

A prophet, then, was one who spoke for God. He was used of God as a direct, authoritative channel to give special divine revelations about contemporary situations and sometimes about the future. Examples of this latter aspect are found in Acts 11:27-28 and 21:8-14.

The second word study we must consider is:

b. Knowledge

The Greek word is *gnōsis,* meaning "to know." This gift was the ability to comprehend and know the mind and will of God. It was not learned knowledge, but rather revealed truth. It was knowledge by the intervention of the Holy Spirit in that which is akin to revelation.

The word refers to the gift of appraisal. It is seen in a miraculous appraisal of things as they truly are. Knowledge is seeing as the Holy Ghost sees. There is a supernatural knowledge and understanding in the gift.

Many illustrations of knowledge are given in the Scriptures. Elijah supernaturally knew all about his greedy servant Gehazi and his scheme for getting riches from Naaman (2 Kings 5:20-27, especially 26). Peter had direct revelation from the Father in heaven as to the knowledge he displayed of who Jesus really was (Matt. 16:13-20, especially 17). Paul divinely understood that the seemingly valid testimony of the young girl concerning the evangelists, their message and God's person, was satanically inspired (Acts 16:16-18, especially 18).

Knowledge was not the product of schooling, therefore. It was the gift of the Holy Spirit. Coming from God directly, knowledge flowed through the gifted person's understanding and tongue. Thus, such knowledge was, like prophecy, as authoritative as the Scriptures in the early church.

One more word needs study, that is:

c. Tongues

The word *glōssa* means "language." As we have seen, in one form or another, this is the word referred to on Pentecost (Acts 2), at Caesarea (Acts 10), in Ephesus (Acts 19), and throughout 1 Corinthians 12, 13 and 14. A tongue could be translated or interpreted. It conveyed a message from heaven in a language other than the native tongue of the speaker.

Thus tongues were tied to the concepts presented with regard to prophecy and knowledge. As the language was supernaturally given, so was the content. The language was in this sense the vehicle used by God to communicate divine truth.

It was inferior as a means to prophecy and knowledge in that the speaker needed to be translated for the sake of those not understanding the language. Thus Paul says:

> I thank my God, I speak with tongues more than ye all: Yet in the church I had rather speak five words with my understanding, that by my voice I might teach others also, than ten thousand words in an unknown tongue (1 Cor. 14:18-19).

The only way in which tongues could be elevated to the same usefulness as these companion gifts was if the individual also translated what he had just said in the foreign language (1 Cor. 14:5). This, of course, would lead to cumbersome verbage unnecessary in the other two and in reality render tongues unnecessary in the first place!

Combined, these three—prophecies, tongues and knowledge—form the subject of 1 Cor. 13:8. Something is going to happen to each of them. None of them (like faith, hope and love) are to abide. They are transient gifts!

Now this brings us to a second interpretive need:

2. A GRAMMAR STUDY

Important grammatical distinctions are introduced in 1 Cor. 13:8. These can be summarized in a preliminary form by the analysis presented in the following chart by Joseph Dillow (12:113).

Spiritual gift	English word for its cessation	Greek verb	Tense	Voice	Meaning
prophecy	cease	katargeo	future	passive	sudden removal, abolish
tongues	be stilled	pauo	future	middle	gradual passing away
knowledge	pass away	katargeo	future	passive	sudden removal, abolish

Keeping this chart in mind can help visualize some of the more technical matter in this grammatical study.

First of all, then, let us deal with the grammar relating to:

a. Prophecy and Knowledge

There are four separate English words used in the Authorized translation of 1 Cor. 13:8-11 to interpret the same Greek word, *katargeō*. This word relates to what God said would happen to prophecy and knowledge. In the Authorized Version the word is found in verse 8, translated as "shall fail" and "vanish away." Verse 10, on the other hand, translates it "done away" while verse 11 has "put away."

Unfortunately the King James scholars seemed to have forgotten that it is the obvious duty of translators to represent and not to improve upon the language of their author. Such, of course, is the problem with many of today's modern translations. Those who have done the translating seem to have felt their job was to transform the original instead of translating it.

In the case of 1 Cor. 13:8, the Greek word is *katargē-thēsontai*. It is the first future passive of *katargeō*, meaning to "render useless," or "to render inoperative." Because it is in the passive voice, this tells us that the action that will produce this condition will be from outside and have the result of rendering the prophecy and knowledge "useless," or "inoperative."

But there is another word used in dealing with:

b. Tongues

This is the Greek word *pauō*, meaning "to cause to cease." In 1 Cor. 13:8 the word is in the middle voice indicative mood. *Pausontai* means that the action will come from within, rather than from without.

The word cease, therefore, holds the idea that tongues would fulfill their function and render themselves inoperative, unneeded, ended. A fair translation might be, "tongues shall make themselves to cease," or "tongues shall automatically cease of themselves." Whichever translation is used, the emphatic message is that tongues shall indeed cease.

The third need for an understanding of this passage is:

3. AN INTERPRETIVE STUDY

The question of when the happenings of verse 8 occur is obviously very important. If they happened in the first century, then tongues have ceased. On the other hand, if they do not happen until the second coming as the charismatics claim, then tongues may indeed be for today.[1] Therefore, our interpretive study is very crucial to the position taken on tongues by neo-Pentecostals.

Although tongues are mentioned in verse 1, the main contribution of the chapter to the contemporary issue is

---

[1] Having said this "tongue in cheek," we need to note that the present passage is not the only one which teaches the temporary nature of tongues. The purpose statement (1 Cor. 14:21-22) makes this abundantly clear, as well as other Scriptures dealing with the "confirming" nature of the sign gifts (Heb. 2:3-4). Furthermore the fact that Christ's promise of "new tongues" was clearly fulfilled in the first century (Mark 16:20), would seem to leave no promise concerning tongues yet to be fulfilled. Thus, we could conclude without 1 Cor. 13:8-12 that tongues have ceased.

in verses 8 to 12. These are the verses which reveal the
when of tongues ceasing as a continuing New Testament
gift of the Spirit. To deal with the question of tongues,
however, one must first of all deal with the question of:

a. When Prophecies and Knowledge are Superseded.

We read concerning these in 1 Cor. 13:8, "Charity
never faileth: but whether there be prophecies, they shall
fail; whether there be tongues, they shall cease; whether
there be knowledge, it shall vanish away." It is necessary for us to take a second look at the meaning of these
words at this point.

It should be noted that the noun *prophēteia*, "prophecy," has two meanings. In our word study earlier we
dealt with the primary meaning which deals with the *act*
of prophesying. But a second interpretation can refer to
the *content* of prophecy. Passages such as Matt. 13:14, 2
Pet. 1:20-21 and Rev. 1:3 refer to prophecy in terms of
content. The same case can be made with regard to
"knowledge."

The question is, in what sense does Paul use the words
prophecies and knowledge in 1 Cor. 13:8? It is most likely that he had the act of prophesying and the act of ut-
tering the words of knowledge in mind. This would
describe what was taking place in the day in which he
was addressing the Corinthians. The act of exercising
these gifts in the church would, therefore, be the
understanding his primary readers would conceive from
his words.

However, there is another sense in which these words
can be used and that describes the product of these gifts.
In this sense they refer to the content produced, rather
than the act of exercising the gift. As the act referred to
verbalization, the content refers to codification. Thus,
prophecy and knowledge eventually came to be the content of written revelation.

However, after each prophecy, or word of knowledge
had been given, what was gathered (the content) was
seen to be only a part of the total revelatory picture. It

was like one piece in the overall jigsaw of God's revelation, the total picture not yet being complete. Paul explains, "For we know in part, and we prophecy in part" (1 Cor. 13:9). The early church, therefore, passed through an intermediate or transitional state, wherein some prophecy and knowledge was known through the act of the gifts being exercised and some through the content of gift-exercise already codified.

The emphasis concerning that early period must be upon the transitional nature of this state of affairs, for Paul quickly moves on to explain further, "But when that which is perfect is come, then that which is in part shall be done away" (1 Cor. 13:10). There would come a time when the last piece of the jigsaw of revelation was put in place. Then there would be no more partial revelations, for they would be swallowed up in the "perfect" (complete) revelation of the Word of God.

The act of prophecy and of speaking a word of knowledge was forever "done away" when the content of these was finally and completely codified. What was produced furnishes God's entire, inspired and inerrant Word to man for all time. Only in the second coming of Christ, when faith shall be sight and when what is revealed in the pages of God's Word shall be swallowed up by the personal, bodily revelation of the actual Person of Christ, shall the codified content of prophecy and knowledge be superseded.

When did the gifts of prophecy and knowledge pass away? As far as the act of their exercise as a gift is concerned, they gradually passed away as the New Testament was written down. Then the very moment the last verse of the book of Revelation was written, all prophecies and knowledge forever passed away. The content of that prophecy and knowledge, on the other hand, has been codified as the Scriptures and is the revelation of God to our hearts and lives till Jesus comes again. Thus, our conclusion must be that these gifts are not in operation today, though we benefit from the *content* of them as found in the Bible.

We are now ready to deal with the question of:

b. When Tongues "Shall Cease"

The question really is, do tongues cease before prophecies and knowledge are rendered inoperative?
Several important details affirm that they do:

First of all there is the change of verbs in verse 8. In
relationship to prophecies and knowledge he uses
katargeō, meaning to "render inoperative, or to
supersede." However, he carefully selects the word *pauō*
to describe what happens to tongues. In the active voice
this term means "to make to cease."

Now why does Paul make this change? It certainly is
not true that he merely wanted to avoid repetition, for
his use of katargeō some four times in these verses
(verses 8, 10 and 11) tells us he did not fear to repeat
himself. No, the conclusion is clear, tongues were viewed
as ceasing "before" the completion of revelation, while
prophecies and knowledge would be rendered inoperative or superseded "by" the completed Scriptures.

A *second* point to be noted is the change of voice Paul
uses in the verbs of verse 8. Both uses of katargeō are in
the future passive voice. However pauō is in the future
middle voice. In the indicative, pauō means "to make to
cease" and is so used in 1 Pet. 3:10, where it is translated
"refrain." "For he that will love life, and see good days,
let him refrain[2] his tongue from evil, and his lips that
they speak no guile." Incidentally the word "tongue" in
this verse is the same one as 1 Cor. 13:8.

Had Paul wanted to say that tongues would be made
to cease by the completion of the Scriptures, he would
most probably have used the active voice. He did not do
so, but instead used the middle voice making the word
simply mean, "to cease of themselves." Thus, a further
conclusion can be reached; while the content of prophecies and knowledge would remain until the completion of the Scriptures, tongues would in the meanwhile
cease in and of themselves.

A *third* point is added immediately by the omission of
tongues in verse 9. Why are prophecies and knowledge
mentioned and tongues are not? Surely it is more than a

---

[2] The word is, pausatō, meaning literally "let him cause to cease."

mere oversight on Paul's part. In verse 10 both knowledge and prophecies are said to be rendered inoperative by "that which is perfect." However, the implication is that tongues will not be in existence to be rendered inoperative when "that which is perfect is come." The conclusion, therefore, is that even before the completion of the canon of Holy Scripture, tongues ceased in and of themselves.

Now this interpretive study brings us logically to the need for:

4. A DEVELOPMENTAL STUDY

Even a preliminary reading of 1 Cor. 13 shows that there is a progression in the chapter. Paul is presenting a development from infancy to maturity, to ultimate (seen in the face to face meeting with Christ). If we are to understand the passage, therefore, we must not only trace this development but also seek to understand the maturation which the apostle has in mind.

Notice first of all, that Paul begins this maturing process:

a. In Infancy

Verse 11 says, "When I was a child, I spake as a child, I understood as a child, I thought as a child" (1 Cor. 13:11). The word used for child is *nēpios*, which is composed of the negative *nē* and *epos*, to speak. Thus the word refers to an infant who has not yet fully developed the ability to speak properly.

The test says that at this period of non-speech, the child verbalizes. *Laleō* is the word and it refers to vocalized sound. What that sound is, is defined by the words describing it. Thus the speech referred to is the speech of a nēpios, a child who cannot yet express himself intelligibly.

More than this, speech patterns are attached to thought patterns. Therefore, says Paul, *ephronoun*—I thought (understood in Authorized Version)—as a nēpios, an infant. The word comes from *phroneō*, meaning to be minded (phrēn, the mind) in a certain way, or to think in a certain pattern. Thus, at the time of which the apostle writes, his thinking process was at the stage of a nēpios, an infant.

In the second place, Paul moves in his development:

b. To Adulthood

He tells us he "became a man." The word is anēr and is used in distinction from infant. Three separate words in the Hebrew describe the Greek anēr:

(a) Naar, a youth, referring to the beginning of maturity. It applies to that period when the child begins to become independent from his parents. Included is the basic idea, "to shake off."

(b) Bachur, the ripened one. Here is a youth who had developed to the stage where he is ready for military service. He is now ready to live life on his own.

(c) Ish, a man. The process is now complete. He is mature physically, mentally and socially. Now the course of life allows him to set up his own home, distinct from his parents, with its own identity.

To become a man, therefore, involved the "shaking off" of childhood. It was becoming independent of parental supervision and support. A man was an entity on his own, dependent upon himself for survival as a mature person.

In this sense, Paul tells us he has moved from nēpios to anēr; from infancy to mature manhood. Hence, He did away with the things of an infant. His speech, his thought patterns, his ability to reason all marked him off as an adult. His own statement is, "when I became a man, I put away childish things" (1 Cor. 13:11).

Now all of this has:

c. Application to the Church

In the early stages, prophecies and tongues and knowledge were necessary. They had a function which had not yet been fulfilled. The gifts, therefore, helped the church to have a firm foundation (Eph. 2:20).

But as the infant body of the church was developing, 1 Cor. 13:9 says that its knowledge was incomplete, partial. The word *merous,* meaning a part or portion of the whole, is coupled with the preposition *ek,* from. Thus, the knowledge and prophecies were parts separated from the whole revelation of God.

Hence, 1 Cor. 13:10 introduces the term, *to teleion,* translated in the Authorized Version by "that which is perfect." Teleion carries the idea of wholeness, of that which is complete. It is the opposite of *ek merous,* that which is but a part of the whole. In other words, verse 11 refers to the completion of God's revelation to mankind, in which the partial is swallowed up by the entire canon of the Holy Scriptures. From that time onward the church had the means of a complete knowledge of all that God had ever said, or would say, by means of "prophecies" and "knowledge." The gifts of prophecy and knowledge, therefore, failed and vanished away (1 Cor. 13:8).

The impact of this was a maturing church coming to the complete, "knowledge of the Son of God, unto a perfect man, unto the measure of the stature of the fulness of Christ" (Eph. 4:13). That word perfect is, *teleion,* complete maturity in fullgrown manhood and the contrast given is, "That we henceforth be no more children, tossed to and fro, and carried about with every wind of doctrine, by the sleight of men, and cunning craftiness, whereby they lie in wait to deceive" (Eph. 4:14). "Children" is the plural of our word nēpios from 1 Cor. 13:11. By the finalized Word of God the church moved from infancy to the maturity of adulthood.

At the same time as the church was maturing:

d. Tongues Were Ceasing

We have already dealt in some depth with the purpose of tongues mentioned in 1 Cor. 14:21-22. As the channels of maturation were converging upon the closing of the canon of the Scriptures, another cataclysmic event occurred. In A.D. 70 the armies of the Roman general Titus destroyed Jerusalem, fulfilling the purpose for which the Bible says tongues were given. Thus tongues ceased in and of themselves, there no longer being a reason for them to continue.

Again, at that same point in history, the church moved from nēpios to anēr, from infancy to manhood. You see, up until that moment, Christianity and Judaism had been twins. The early believers still worshiped, prayed and fellowshipped in the synagogue. They still considered themselves Jews who believed on their Messiah. Indeed to the world at large Christianity was just another Jewish sect. Thus, Farrar in speaking of the destruction of Jerusalem refers to Sulpicius Severus, "who is probably quoting the very words of Tacitus, [stating that] Titus formed the deliberate purpose to destroy Christianity and Judaism in one blow, believing that if the Jewish root were torn up the Christian branch would soon perish." (14:326)

But, with the destruction of Jerusalem in A.D. 70, the church moved out of its childhood home. It got a separate identity and became distinct in its existence. No longer was it merely another branch of Judaism, but a completely separate religion. Furthermore, this religion could continue and grow without the focus of a Jewish temple in Jerusalem, or the umbrella of a Jewish religious system. Manhood had been reached and with it another reason for dropping off the gift which marked its infancy, the gift of tongues.

As the destruction of Jerusalem and the severing of dependence upon Judaism mark the time of tongues passing, so the closing of the canon of Scripture with the writing of the last book does also. The final book of the Bible to be written was, "The Revelation of Jesus Christ, which God gave unto him, to shew unto his servants things which must shortly come to pass; and he sent and signified it by his angel unto his servant John" (Rev. 1:1). When the last chapter of that book was being written, our Lord gave His unyielding warning across the totality of the Scriptures:

> For I testify unto every man that heareth the words of the prophecy of this book, If any man shall add unto these things, God shall add unto him the plagues that are written in this book: And if any man shall take away from the words of the book of this pro-

phecy, God shall take away his part out of the book of life, and out of the holy city, and from the things which are written in this book (Rev. 22:18-19)."

There would be no more partial revelations given by prophecies or knowledge. They had forever been superseded.

But wait! As we have noted at length in our interpretive study of 1 Cor. 13:9-10, tongues would already have ceased when partial prophecies and knowledge ended. Thus, we can say that the period in which tongues were ceasing in and of themselves was approximately that between A.D. 70 and A.D. 100. By the time these thirty years had passed the Biblical gift of tongues had ceased.

When Paul wrote 1 Corinthians chapters 12, 13 and 14, about the year A.D. 55, tongues still had purpose. They were a sign to the Jews that Isaiah's prophecy was about to be fulfilled. The infant church was a sibling in its childhood home. No one was, therefore, to forbid speaking in tongues.

However, after Jerusalem's fall and before the Scripture's completion, the Biblical gift of tongues ceased, never to be heard again from the lips of the matured church (1 Cor. 13:11). With manhood reached, heralded by perfected knowledge (i.e. understanding) and prophecy (i.e. thought), the childish things were forever put away. To revert to these would herald a tragedy; a breakdown in manhood and a pathetic regression to infancy. Tongues are not for the church today, for they have ceased.

With this the history of the church agrees. In an article entitled, "The Gift of Tongues in the Post Apostolic Church," Cleon L. Rogers Jr. analyses their use between the years 100 and 400 A.D. After dealing with the testimony of the Apostolic Fathers, Justin Martyr, Irenaeus, Tertullian, Origen, Chrysostom and others, he concludes:

> After examining the testimony of the early Christian leaders whose ministry represents practically every area of the Roman Empire from approximately A.D.

100 to 400, it appears that the miraculous gifts of the first century died out and were no longer needed to establish Christianity. Furthermore, it is very evident that even if the gift were in existence, in spite of all the testimony to the contrary, it was neither widespread nor the normal Christian experience. The only clear reference to anything resembling the phenomena is connected with the heretic Montanus and those influenced by his erroneous use of the Spirit. All of the evidence points to the truth of Paul's prophecy when he says, "tongues shall cease (77:143)."

Let us not be misled by those who would try to revive gifts which have fulfilled their purpose and which, by the testimony of Scripture and history, ceased when that purpose was fulfilled within the first century.

We come now to the fifth need facing us in seeking to determine the meaning of this passage, that is a study to gather the foregoing together:

5. AN EXPLANATORY STUDY

Verses 9 to 13 in 1 Cor. 13 clarify and answer for us the question, *Why?* Why have tongues ceased? First of all, they explain to us:

a. The Fragmentary Versus the Complete

In verse 9 is a clear statement that the prophecy and knowledge of verse 8 were but partial, fragmentary revelations. Paul says, "we know in part, and we prophesy in part" (1 Cor. 13:9). We might also note again in this text that tongues is pointedly not mentioned. Apparently they would no longer be there when the action of verse 10 came to pass.

According to verse 10 the partial would give way to the "perfect," for "when that which is perfect is come, then that which is in part shall be done away." *Teleion* means to be full grown, complete, mature. Thus, when that having to do with God's revelation to man is complete, the fragmentary revelations would come to an end. So, with the closing of the canon of the Holy Scriptures,

God's complete, final "perfect" revelation came in and prophecy and knowledge were rendered useless and inoperative.

Secondly, these verses explain to us:

b. The Childish Verses the Manly

Verse 11 introduces us to this thought in relation to tongues. "When I was a child, I spake as a child, I understood as a child, I thought as a child: but when I became a man, I put away childish things." Please remember that language is merely the verbalizing of one's thoughts and denotes one's level of understanding. Tongues, in the early church, were thus like infancy language to a man.

Remember also, that Corinthians are two of Paul's earliest letters, preceded only by Thessalonians and Galatians. Afterwards he wrote Romans, Colossians, Philemon, Ephesians, Philippians, 1 Timothy, Titus and 2 Timothy, yet *none of these* mentions speaking in tongues. Apparently this was the first sign gift to cease and it ceased almost immediately, for it belonged to the infancy of the church.

When we hear a little baby speaking in childish language, we think it is cute. We expect simple, unintelligible gibberish, understandable only as baby talk. All the goo-goos, ma-mas, da-das and so on are most acceptable—for a baby in its first years of life. This is normal!

However, when because of some mental breakdown a full-grown man reverts to babyhood, things are different. He slobbers and slurs out his mono-syllables. Unintelligible sounds herald the short-circuit in his brain. Do we still stand back and applaud? Do we still think its cute? No! We think it is pathetic! Why? Because men are expected to have "put away childish things." What is normal in infancy is abnormal in adulthood.

So, for the church to revert to tongues, is to revert to babyhood. Paul is, therefore, telling the Corinthians even at that early date to recognize tongues for what they really are. The time was fast approaching when they would have to grow up, put away their babytalk and become full-grown men!

Thirdly, these verses explain.

C. The Picture Versus the Person

In 1 Cor. 13:11-12 we read:

> When I was a child, I spake as a child, I understood as a child, I thought as a child: but when I became a man, I put away childish things.
> For now we see through a glass, darkly; but then face to face: now I know in part; but then shall I know even as also I am known.

Have you noticed the ever widening circles of explanation? First the completion of revelation—the Bible. Second the completion of maturity—the Personality. Now the completion of expectation—the Lord.

Complete as the Bible is in its revelation of God's truth, we still must "walk by faith, not by sight" (2 Cor. 5:7). "Now we see through a glass darkly"—His image is there. As we study the Word, "we all, with open face beholding as in a glass the glory of the Lord, are changed into the same image from glory to glory even as by the Spirit of the Lord" (2 Cor. 3:18).

Yet, with all that the Word reveals through its pages, we find ourselves still fitting in to 1 Pet. 1:8, "Whom having not seen, ye love; in whom, though now ye see Him not, yet believing, ye rejoice with joy unspeakable and full of glory." The Bible is wonderful, our unfailing guide to Him; maturity in Christ is precious, making us like Him; but His return is our hope, we shall see Him face to face and know Him even as He knows us. Oh, what a great, grand, glorious, overwhelming day that will be; when faith shall be sight, and we shall be forever with the Lord!

What then should be our present response? Realizing that tongues have indeed ceased in and of themselves, we should be striving towards perfection (i.e. manhood, maturity, full-growth). We should seek to fulfill 2 Tim. 2:15 in our relationship to the Word of God. Further, we should seek not to be among those of 1 Cor. 3:1-3, or those of Heb. 5:12-14, who were still children and needed to grow up. Our aim should be that we might, "stand perfect and complete in all the will of God" (Col. 4:12) and selflessly strive also, "that we may present every man perfect in Christ Jesus" (Col. 1:28). Our benediction, therefore, will be:

Now the God of peace, that brought again from the dead our Lord Jesus, that great shepherd of the sheep, through the blood of the everlasting covenant, Make you perfect in every good work to do his will, working in you that which is well pleasing in his sight, through Jesus Christ; to whom be glory for ever and ever. Amen (Heb. 13:20-21).

6

THE RETURN OF TONGUES
ITS SOURCE

No other religious phenomenon has invaded modern Christianity as has that of tongues. It is the prominent watershed for all the other characteristics of the neo-Pentecostal movement. Without it, the rest of *the gifts* would not have the appeal which they enjoy amongst charismatic Christians.

Concerning this claimed revival of the New Testament gifts, Paul Van Gorder expresses our feeling well.

> From certain quarters has come the plea for a truce in the controversy concerning tongues.[1] We too desire harmony among the children of God, but it must not be gained at the expense of the teaching of the Bible. Let us be reminded that the apostle Paul confronted Peter on at least one occasion, and we hear Paul say, "I withstood him to the face, because he was to be blamed" (Gal. 2:11). Since it fails in rightly dividing the Word, ignores Biblical history, and exalts experience above doctrine, we must carefully examine the charismatic movement (61:35).

The examination of this present chapter will be against the backdrop of the contemporary history of the movement's use of *tongues.*

When we thus examine the tongues movement, we discover:

---

[1] See "A Truce Proposal for the Tongues Controversy" by Clark H. Pinnock and Grant R. Osborne in *Christianity Today*, October 8th, 1971, page 6 for an example of this.

A. The Methodology is Suspect

As with the variety of techniques which converge to belie the spontaneity of the movement as a whole,[2] so also the methodology would appear to have a clearly carnal base. For example one can easily discover of tongues-speaking that:

1. IT IS A LEARNED RESPONSE

Years ago Joseph Smith, the founder of the Mormon cult, taught his disciples to speak in tongues with this instruction, "Arise upon your feet, speak or make some sound, continue to make sounds of some kind, and the Lord will make a tongue or language of it" (37:53). To him tongues was a learned response.

Many non-charismatics would be shocked to learn that today's neo-Pentecostal movement has not progressed beyond this psychology. Famous charismatic Oral Roberts writes:

> As that welling up comes again to you, open your mouth and submit your tongues to God. Lift up your voice but do not attempt to speak in your own language. You cannot speak in two languages at the same time. You may actually hear or see words. Or you may feel something moving in your mouth.
>
> I could have spoken in tongues a long time before I did had someone instructed me. Too often wrong instructions are given persons preparing to receive the baptism with the Holy Ghost (32:35).

Clearly, his methodology has not progressed far beyond that of Joseph Smith.

Catholic charismatic writer Stephen Clark likewise speaks of tongues as a learned phenomenon.

> If the community we are part of has learned to yield to the gift tongues, when we are baptized in the

---

[2]See pages 122ff. for a discussion of the slick Madison Avenue sales technique employed by full gospel mens' fellowships, contemporary charismatic radio and television programs, plus the many rallies—large and small—which mimic these techniques.

Spirit, we will speak in tongues much more readily (53:19).

In our community, it is usual for people to pray in tongues when they are prayed with to be baptized in the Spirit (if they have been properly instructed and prepared), and the few exceptions pray in tongues within a matter of days or weeks (53:25).

Apparently the same methodology is used in the Catholic wing of the movement.

But what is meant by *learning* to speak in tongues? Perhaps we should let Don Basham, a modern charismatic highpriest, give us the actual instructions he has used with many groups of seekers. The quote is lengthy but utterly revealing.

Now the first thing I want to tell you is this: You can sit back and relax, for you can receive the baptism in the Holy Spirit and you can speak in tongues. It is in your power to do all you have to do. The same faith that enabled you to receive Jesus Christ as your Savior is all the faith you need to receive the baptism in the Holy Spirit with speaking in tongues. After all, the baptism, in one sense, is simply receiving more of Jesus. It's meeting Him in a new dimension, as the Baptizer in the Holy Spirit as John the Baptist spoke of Him in Luke 3:16. There is no reason why everyone of you ... will not receive the Holy Spirit and be praising God in a new and unknown tongue within a very few minutes. So relax and be confident. It will happen.

I want to take a few minutes to explain the procedure we are going to follow.... The first step is receiving the Holy Spirit within; the second is to manifest the Spirit's presence by praising God in a new or "unknown" tongue. Again, let me make it clear; everyone of you can do this. It is within your power, once you understand what is required of you, to receive the Holy Spirit and to speak in tongues.

Now when the prayer for you to receive is offered (and I'm simply going to pray one single prayer aloud in behalf of all of you, asking the Lord Jesus to baptize you in the Holy Spirit and to enable you to praise Him in a new, supernatural way), immediately after the ending of the prayer, I will ask you to do a very simple thing. I will ask you to open your mouth and breathe in or drink in a deep, full breath of air....

All right, that's the first step; "breathing in" the Holy Spirit and having faith that He's coming in. And that is the easiest of the two steps. But we don't want to stop there; we also want you to have the Scriptural confirmation of the Holy Spirit's presence in your life in a new way by having you receive the manifestation of speaking in tongues. Again, let me tell you, relax! You can do this. You can receive the evidence of speaking in tongues. It is in your power to do it. Let me explain what I mean.

Speaking in tongues—which is the scriptural proof or sign that you have received the baptism in the Holy Spirit—is a miracle; it is supernatural. I believe we are all agreed on that. But let me remind you again that miracles are composed of two parts; man's part (which is natural) and God's part (which is supernatural). One of the best Scriptural examples of this truth is the miracle of Peter's walking on the water, recorded in Matt. 14. You remember the story....

So when the time comes for you to speak in tongues, be ready! After I have prayed the prayer in your behalf, and immediately after you have opened your mouth and breathed in the Holy Spirit, I'm going to tell you to let that breath out. Only, do not let it out silently; but put the sound of your voice behind it. Just begin to praise God with the sound of your voice as if you never learned the English language. God already knows you can speak English, so don't even attempt to praise Him in your natural language. If you start to pray or praise in English, you'll only have to stop before you can begin to speak in tongues. Even the Holy Spirit cannot make you speak two languages at once....

Now when I give the word for you to open your mouth and begin to praise God, I know from experience that some of you will receive tongues instantly. Others of you will be a little hesitant to begin to speak. But just gather your courage and begin to speak anyway. Just babble out whatever pops into your mind and whatever you feel on your lips and tongue. And once you begin, keep it up. Don't stop. Let the language flow out freely. If you can speak five words or syllables, you can speak five thousand. The Holy Spirit has an unlimited vocabulary.

And another thing. When you start to speak, don't worry about what it sounds like. It may sound like Chinese, like Polynesian, like the notes of the musical scale, or even like baby-talk. What it sounds like is the Holy Spirit's business. Your business is just to speak out. The Holy Spirit will give you words and syllables in the language He wants you to pray in. Don't get concerned if the person sitting next to you is praying with different sounds from yours. Don't examine it, just do it! ...

Now, I believe it's time to pray. Relax, and get ready for what is going to happen. You are about to move into a deep and wonderful new dimension of Christian experience, even though it happens in what may seem to be a strange and foolish way. Never mind. It's real. It's supernatural. And believe me, after today, your life will never be the same! Let's pray.

Dear Jesus, we thank you for the promise of your Holy Spirit today. We thank you that you are pouring out your Holy Spirit with the blessing of speaking in tongues. Lord, we ask you to honor the faith of all the people in this room, and to confirm your word in them. We ask you right now, Lord Jesus, to baptize everyone in this room with your Holy Spirit, and enable them to praise you with a language they never learned but which is pleasing to you. Thank you, Lord Jesus, Amen.

Now every one of you, "Receive ye the Holy Ghost" and praise God in other tongues! Amen!

All right, open your mouth and take in that deep breath of air. Breathe in deeply and as you do, believe the Holy Spirit is coming in. That's right! Good!

Now, let that breath out, and begin to praise God with the sound of your voice, and receive the utterance the Holy Spirit gives (2:54-64)!

Probably the "instructor" sincerely wishes to be of help to those desiring the *baptism,* however, his practice of psychological manipulation amply illustrates the learned response factor in charismatic methodology.

A friend tells of a Caribbean Cruise on which he inadvertently found himself amongst some 300 charismatics, led by some of the "top guns of the movement" in the United States. On the Sunday, the group commandeered the ballroom for a meeting led by Demos Shakarian, founder of the Full Gospel Businessmen's Fellowship.[3] My friend went along to be an eyewitness of the happening.

Instructions were given for those present to form a circle with finger tips only touching. Then they were told to begin to "loosen up" by vigorously shaking their arms which soon began to tingle. Finally, they were directed to begin saying, "Jesus ... Jesus ... Jesus," over and over, louder and louder, faster and faster.

Soon people were speaking in tongues. Some were dropping physically to the floor in a trance-like state. All seemed involved in an ecstatic frame of mind. My friend ended his account by saying simply, "I think they hypnotized themselves!" It was a learned response produced by the fulfilled instructions of the leader.

Surely Morris is right when he differentiates the teaching of Paul, as found in 1 Corinthians chapters 12, 13 and 14, from the modern movement's indoctrinations, saying:

> The contrast of Paul's descriptions and instructions regarding tongues in these chapters with the present-day phenomenon as usually practiced is quite sharp. One can hardly avoid the conclusion that

---

[3] By the way, according to Eric Fife, "It is interesting to note that Demos Shakarian, the founder of the Full Gospel Businessmens' Fellowship, insists that he has no gift of speaking or healing, but believes his gift is that of 'helps'." (15:139)

the Biblical gift of tongues is not the same thing at all as its modern namesake (28:130).

Rather than a learned response, Biblical tongues was a sovereign gift (1 Cor. 12:13) which was not meant for everybody (1 Cor. 12:30)—even in Paul's day!

Another alarming factor in the methodology used by those who teach tongues are for today is that:

2. IT BY-PASSES THE INTELLECT

What I am now charging is that the modern achievement of tongues necessitates that the seeker lay aside that which most marks his personhood, namely his mind and thought control. This is a part of the instruction given continually amongst charismatics. For example Clark writes:

> One reason why the gift of tongues is so important for modern Americans is that it is easier for them to yield to the Holy Spirit in tongues than it is in English. They can more easily overcome their inhibitions by by-passing their minds (which is what happens in tongues—1 Cor. 14:14) than through their minds (53:28).

Note well, that inhibitions brought about by mind control can only be broken, according to Clark, through a "by-passing" of one's mind.

When giving his instructions concerning "How to Receive the Gift of the Holy Ghost," Oral Roberts also pleads for this by-passing of one's intelligence. "Next, your will is involved. Your intellect is partially by-passed for the moments you will be speaking in tongues (32:39)." Then he goes on to explain:

> Our intellect is one of the great forces that makes us different from all other creatures. We are thankful for our intellect. This is the age of reason. Our intellect is that against which we struggle the longest. We do not want to submit it. But God is Spirit and He cannot be reasoned out. Years ago I was almost beside myself trying to reason this out. Paul reached

a point where he had to bend his intellect, and if he could bend his giant intellect we can certainly afford to bend ours. At times he had to quit talking in his own language and quit thinking in his own mind. He simply prayed in tongues and let his spirit reach upward to God. As this was valid and valuable for Paul, it is a precious privilege for us also.

When we pray we sometimes reach a place in our minds where we cannot express what is in our spirits, what is in our total inner man. We have to by-pass our mind and make it inactive for the moment. The mind slips into the background during the moments we are praying in tongues and remains in a state of neutrality (32:42).

Apart from drawing attention to the fact that Paul distinctly tells us that he would not "by-pass," or "bend his intellect" (1 Cor. 14:14-15), let me just comment that Roberts sets forth the neo-Pentecostal emphasis on this matter.

Modern charismatics might be shocked to learn that in this point they are directly paralleling the heathen mystery religions of Paul's day. In fact, one of the key characteristics of their tongues-speaking was the lack of connection with their mental processes. In other words, they prayed without their minds being engaged. Thus, there was produced the "muttering of words, or sounds without interconnection or meaning," as part of the idol worship at Corinth (21:722).

How different is the emphasis of Scripture with regard to one's mind control. One word only, together with its five derivatives, is used in the New Testament to denote soundness of mind. It is the word *sōphrōn*. This term is applied to words (Acts 26:25), thoughts (Rom. 12:3), service (2 Cor. 5:13), women (1 Tim. 2:9), motherhood (1 Tim. 2:15), mind (2 Tim. 1:7), office (Titus 1:8), old age (Titus 2:2), marriage (Titus 2:5), youth (Titus 2:6), conduct (Titus 2:11-12), and to the end (1 Pet. 4:7). Combined, they emphasize sanity throughout life by advocating complete control of one's mind at all times!

You see, the overall stress of the New Testament is upon a person being in control of himself and not "bypassing" his God given mental processes and intellect. As Schofield wrote:

> Much of the high-flown language of the present day in connection with this is contrary to the Word of God, which never asks us to lay aside our sound mind, our sobriety, our self-control, our reasonableness, and our judgment; but to exercise these faculties in accordance with His Word (38:123).

The tragedy of the modern tongues movement is that they have not yet learned this, otherwise their exponents would not be enjoining such anti-Biblical methodology.

We come now to a second discovery with regard to the contemporary tongues movement.

B. THE PRODUCT IS ILLUSION

Often it is the product that charismatics point to in seeking to verify the validity of their experience. They tell us that the baptism with the Holy Spirit has produced speaking with tongues in their lives. Certainly the methodology reviewed produces something but it is certainly not Biblical tongues.

The product of neo-Pentecostalism has been:

1. ANALYZED BY EXPERTS

Remember, from all we have learned about the Biblical gift of tongues, it involved speaking in a *real language.* It may have been foreign to the speaker but it was not to some hearers at least. The need for an interpreter only occurred when those were present to whom the language was unintelligible, because foreign.

With this in mind, it would seem reasonable that today's tongues—if Biblical—could be verified as real by language experts. Can this be done? For the most part *no.*[4] The great preponderance of what passes for tongues has been analyzed as non-language.

---

[4] We shall deal with the exceptions in considering demonism and cryptomnesia as causes for actual languages spoken.

Take, for example, the analysis of William E. Welmers, Professor of African Languages at the University of California in Los Angeles:

We do know something about representative languages of every known language family in the world. I am by no means unique among descriptive linguists in having had direct, personal contact with well over a hundred languages representing a majority of the world's language families, and in having studied descriptions of languages of virtually every reported type. If a glossolalic (i.e., one who professes to speak in unknown tongues in the Holy Spirit's power) were speaking in any of the thousand languages of Africa, there is about a 90 per cent chance that I would know it in a minute. Now, I have also had the opportunity of making a sympathetic study of an alleged instance of speaking in tongues. And I must report without reservation that my sample does not sound like a language structurally....

The consonants and vowels do not all sound like English (the glossolalic's native language), but the intonation patterns are so completely American English that the total effect is a bit ludicrous. My sample includes an "interpretation." At the most generous estimate, the glossolalic utterance includes ten or eleven "sentences" or stretches of possibly meaningful speech. But the "interpretation" involves no less than fourteen distinct and independent ideas. There simply can be no match between the "tongue" and the "interpretation." I am told that Dr. E. A. Nida of the American Bible Society has reported similar impressions of glossolalic recordings. Our evidence is still admittedly limited, but from the viewpoint of a Christian linguist the modern phenomenon of glossolalia would appear to be a linguistic fraud and monstrosity, given even the most generous interpretation of 1 Cor. 12-14 (78:127-8).

Surely such an analysis by so distinguished a linguist ought to give pause to think, before labelling modern tongues as bona fide.

Then, of course, there is Dr. Eugene A. Nida's study just mentioned. Dr. Nida is one of the outstanding linguists of the day. His analysis involved tongues recorded on tape and played before the Toronto Institute of Linguistics. Present were linguists representing over 150 aboriginal languages in more than twenty-five countries, a good cross section of world language experience. His findings were as follows:

1. Each breath group had the resemblance of a chanted phrase.
2. The vowels used were almost exclusively *i*, *a* and *o*.
3. The consonants showed a remarkable lack of symmetry.
4. There was a "very high repetition of individual sounds and syllables ... a pronounced tendency towards recurring sequences ... This type of distribution is entirely abnormal in linguistic structure."
5. The complete lack of "paralinquistic" features, e.g., pauses, hesitations, "stumbling" in speech, obvious mistakes, and corrective repetitions, is interesting, for this shows quite conclusively that the production of the speech is not under any conscious control, except in matters of beginning, stopping, speed of utterance and the degree of loudness (80:7).

Coming out of this careful analysis was Dr. Nida's conclusion:

The types of inventory and distributions would indicate clearly that this recording bears no resemblance to any actual language which has ever been treated by linguists. It is, therefore, so highly improbable that this is a human language that one can say with a most complete confidence that we must rule out any possibility of Dr. X's having acquired the actual speech of any people. If then, it is not a human language, what is it? One can only say that it is a form of "ecstatic speech." ... On the basis of what I have learned about this type of phenomena of "tongues" in other parts of the world, apparently there is the same tendency to employ one's own inventory of sounds, in nonsense combinations, but with simulated "foreign" features. At least in West Africa and Latin America the types of glossolalia employed seemed to fit into this description (80:7).

Again a conclusion that contemporary tongues are not languages, as we have seen the Biblical occurrences were.

Walter A. Wolfram analyzed glossolalic from eight informants. He examined these from the viewpoint of structural linguistics and discovered that it depended upon the language background of the speaker as to which phonemes or speech patterns were used. Each had similarities including the excessive use of the vowel *a* and of open syllables. Also they tended to end breath groups in vowels—often the same ones. Frequent repetition of words and clauses, one more than ten times and two others as many as twenty times. His conclusion from these findings was that "it is highly improbable that glossolalists are speaking an unlearned non-native tongue" (82:91).

Another recorded analysis was carried out at the invitation of noted charismatic, John Sherrill. He invited David Scott, religious book editor for McGraw-Hill, and six linguists attached to fully accredited educational institutions to listen to some tapes of charismatic tongues-speaking. Of those six specialists, two were expert in modern languages, three in ancient languages, and one in language structure. Later Sherrill reported the results:

> As I put on the first tape, each man leaned forward, straining to catch every syllable. Several took notes. But at no time did I see a face light up with recognition. I played another tape, and then another. For the better part if an hour we listened to one prayer after another spoken "in the Spirit." And when, at last, we came to the end, I looked around and asked, "Well, Gentlemen?" Six heads shook in the negative. Not

one had heard a language which he could identify (40:5).

And how does Sherrill account for this? It's simple, he claims that while tongues may not be *spoken* in a known language, they are often *heard* in a known language! Maybe this is one of those times when the charismatics want us to by-pass our intellects.

Another explanation sometimes given to explain the illusion of the product is that these tongues are:

2. HEAVENLY LANGUAGES

Mainly this is based upon 1 Cor. 13:1, "Though I speak with the tongues of men and of angels, and have not charity, I am become as sounding brass, or a tinkling cymbal." The ordinary language spoken is said to be the tongue of men. However, when tongues are spoken, then it is the language of angels. Thus, the tongues speaker is speaking in a language not known on earth!

It must be noted here that when Paul uses the expression "tongues—of angels," he is employing a method of emphasis. There is no thought of a special, literal, heavenly language being in view. He is merely using contrasting hyperbole to illustrate all possible extremes of language.

By the way, have you ever asked yourself what is the language of angels? Without exception, any time they are heard to speak in the Bible, they use human language that men can understand. The fact is that the greater preponderance of these instances were in Hebrew. Can that be the language of heaven!

On a more serious note, in Matt. 6:7 Christ taught His disciples to avoid meaningless repetition in prayer. He contrasted how they were to pray with the way the heathen pray, saying, "But when ye pray, use not vain repetitions, as the heathen do: for they think that they shall be heard for their much speaking." The word translated *repetitions* is the Greek, *battalogēsētte.*

There are two parts to this word, *batta* which is merely a sound rather than a word, and *logeō* meaning "to speak." Together the word has the idea of "to babble, or to speak without thinking." What Jesus is saying is, "Don't say, 'batta, batta, batta, batta,' when you pray" (12:22). Don't pray in meaningless sounds!

Can it be that this text has a message for those charismatics who laud tongues as the heavenly language of prayer? Would the Holy Spirit cause a Christian to pray in unknown, repetitious syllables, making him do what Jesus taught us not to do? Is the Holy Spirit the author of battalogēsētte? Surely not, unless He is the author of the heathen practice with which Christ contrasted the disciples praying. If modern tongues is a language, we can be sure that it is not the language of heaven.

The question obviously arises also, concerning what might be called:

3. MISSIONARY TONGUES

If Biblical tongues (which, as we have seen, were actual languages in which men could communicate with foreigners in the dialect of their birth) have been revived today, why is there still a need for missionary language study? Shaw relates that in the early days of Pentecostalism:

> It was first thought to be a gift of a foreign tongue, and many, believing that they could speak the language of the heathen, went to the field only to find out that they could not speak the language. The leaders of the movement have changed their attitude, and now speak of it as a heavenly language given as the evidence of the baptism of the Spirit (39:342).

Why is this so?

When Paul spoke the words of 1 Cor. 14:18, he probably did so as the greatest missionary statesman of all time. He was uniquely endowed by God to minister the Gospel in every land to which he went. It may well be that the tongues to which he refers was the supernatural gift of language to communicate the Gospel to each of the linguistic groups to which he would minister.

In this light William J. Sweeting states:

It is interesting to consider that we do not find reference to the use of tongues in the pastoral epistles. That gift was transitional in nature, when the early church was becoming established, and when missionaries and evangelists had neither time nor opportunity to study language. Today, even those cults which most vehemently claim gifts of tongues in their church sessions send their missionaries to language school to "study" the language of the field to which they choose to go (42:121)!

It is easy to speak of a restored gift of tongues but difficult to verify it in the crucible of missionary enterprise.

A third area of examination of the tongues movement leads us to believe that:

C. THE DANGER IS REAL

I have used the word "danger" in the singular because, for the present thought, all that I will say is attributed to a singular source. It seems to me that there is a real danger facing today's charismatics. If tongues are not Biblical, then they are produced from some source other than the Holy Spirit. Later I shall deal with the possible psychological source, but for now I am warning of the danger of a demonic source.

David A. Clemens issues the following warning:

Satan is busy in the lives of Christians and seeks to produce bickering, backbiting, lack of love, self-centeredness, lethargy, and other malicious characteristics among believers. Is it impossible to think that he could be responsible for a phenomenon that causes division among believers in such a matter as the tongues question? Could not he be involved in a phenomenon that side-tracks believers from the specific revealed program of God for their lives? Instead of being controlled by the Spirit of God and being conformed to the image of Christ as the fruit of the Spirit is produced as God intended, many have become preoccupied and consequently sidetracked with tongues. This gift is the least important of all the gifts; a gift the Bible strongly suggests is not for our day. Satan has gained a great victory if he can divert the believers' attention to something as debatable and apparently unimportant as tongues. Not everything that smacks of the miraculous is of God. See Exod. 7:11, 22; 8:7; Matt. 7:22, 23 (9:320).

Such a warning is worthy of the reader's pause to think. If tongues are not of God, of whom are they?

There is a real danger that in seeking this "ceased" gift, the quest can lead the seeker into:

1. YIELDING TO THE OCCULT

I am not barging in where angels fear to tread in this matter. All thinking people, within and without the charismatic movement, will readily see the wisdom in this warning. Remember, we are cautioned in 1 John 4:1, "Beloved, believe not every spirit, but try the spirits whether they are of God: because many false prophets are gone out into the world." There is the Spirit of God and there is the spirit of antichrist.

Now having said this, all of us need to be aware that tongues is not solely a product of the Pentecostal and neo-Pentecostal movement. *The Encyclopaedia Britannica,* for example, cites numerous instances of speaking with tongues amongst pagan cults (13:75). Surely such a fact should give all sincere believers in Christ cause to be concerned, since tongues-speaking is obviously not simply a charismatic phenomenon.

In his excellent book, *Speaking in Tongues,* Joseph Dillow has documented his sources for a whole list of illustrations of occult use of tongues. He states:

> People who have no connection at all with Christianity speak in tongues. D.C. Graham tells of a girl in the Szechwan province of China who was possessed by demons and "began to utter words incoherently." Edward Langston says that in East Africa many persons possessed by demons speak fluently in Swahili or English, although under normal circumstances they do not understand either language. Junod reports that among the Thonga people of Africa,

when a demon is being exorcised the person sings a curative song which he himself composes. Usually the songs are in the Zulu tongue. Even if the person does not know this language, it is claimed that he will be able to use it "by a kind of miracle of tongues." ... Today, ecstatic speech is found among the Mohammedans, and the Eskimos of Greenland. Non-Christian alchemists of the middle ages were reported to have spoken in tongues. This causes them to be popularly feared as men skilled in sorcery. The Bwiti cult among the Fang people of the Gabon Republic has been observed speaking in tongues. The parapsychology laboratory of the University of Virginia Medical School reports incidents of occult speaking in tongues. A Turkish actress claims she learns the "language of Jakosta" from a black man she sees in her dreams (12:172, 173).

Charismatic Christians have no corner on the market as far as this phenomenon is concerned.

The editor of the *Alliance Witness* warns us of the danger of occult invasion through persistence in these matters, when he says:

In spiritism there is the spurious and ridiculous, to be sure, but there is also the genuinely supernatural. Exorcism seems to be as old as the human family. We read of it among the "magicians" of Egypt (Ex. 7 and following), and in the "lying spirits" that led King Ahab to destruction (1 Kings 22). The Bible declares plainly "that in the latter times some shall depart from the faith, giving heed to seducing spirits, and doctrines of devils" (1 Tim. 4:1).

To the Christian insistent upon having some particular gift of the Spirit, and thus rejecting the sovereignity of the Holy Spirit, there can be the dreadful reality of the gift of tongues by demonic power. I have known such.

This phenomenon is also known to exist among heathen peoples. A man who was born and reared on the border of Tibet tells of hearing Tibetan monks speak in English while performing in their ritual dances. They would quote from Shakespeare and use profanity like drunken sailors. They would also speak in German or French, or in languages unknown. Quite recently a retired missionary of the China Island Mission told of the same experience.

Demonism is a dreadful reality to be faced and feared lest, for lack of discernment and teaching, it becomes one's own experience (80:6).

The instances on record are multitudinous, and the seeker after this ceased gift lays himself open to real danger.

Recently a friend recounted some recollections of his youth. He had been born into a home where his parents were avowed spiritualists. Indeed his father (and possibly his mother) was a medium. Each member of the family had a "spirit-guide," who acted both as a source of comfort and as a guide in life. This guide was supposed to be the spirit of a deceased individual. His personal spirit-guide was an Indian girl name named Snowflake.

In meetings, before giving an address the father would speak in tongues. His spirit-guide was a Zulu male, and the father would take on the vocal characteristics of this spirit. Sometimes another medium present would claim to see this Zulu spirit standing beside the speaker and invariably would describe him as a tall, powerful individual. The action of "speaking in Zulu" indicated to all present that the spirit-guide was now in control and was communicating through the speaker.

Obviously speaking in tongues does not necessarily prove the presence of the Holy Spirit. Other spirits are abroad in our world, and they are deceivers. It is wonderful to read, "in malice be ye children," yet it is necessary at the same time to emphasize the second part of Paul's admonition, "but in understanding be men" (1 Cor. 14:20). The word is *teleion,* full grown or mature. We must not allow ourselves to be lead into matters contrary to God's will, as little children would be led along by the hand. Rather must we use the totality of our spiritually matured "understanding" to guard from Satanic deception.

Related to this unintentional yielding to the occult is the danger of:

2. PRODUCING EVIL

Most charismatic writers speak rapturously of the "release in the Spirit" that occurs in the "baptism," and subsequent "tongues." Without exception this wonderful feeling is attributed to the work of God. It is said to be evidence that the promised gift of the Spirit had indeed been given. Now such reasoning is immediately suspect, because it subtly shifts the basis for judgment from the objective truth of the Bible to the subjective feelings of experience.

It is important to note, therefore, that there is another possible interpretation of such an experience. Bryant, in discussing "glossolalia" as "for the most part" being non-communicative, unknown tongue, states:

> I say for the "most part," because in certain isolated instances some in the "glossolalia" movement have been found to be speaking in languages unknown to them. One adherent, for example, is said to have been found to be cursing in ancient Coptic and another denying the deity of Christ in a modern African dialect (7:72)

Such instances are enough to give warning *not* to automatically attribute to God that which is obviously seen to be the work of the devil when the real facts are known.

In his very thoughtful analysis of charismatic phenomena at the earlier part of this century, A. T. Schofield, a medical doctor in England, documented a number of cases where tongues produced evil. For example, he writes of a pastor in India who supposedly "received the baptism" in a certain meeting.

> Gradually, as I watched the process, the pastor became more and more under the influence, and at last lost control and fell over. Then he knelt up again

and began to pray in an ecstacy, but without any coherence.

I heard him repeat rapidly the word preaching (prasangam) in Tamil many times, and then at last he seemed to lose all knowledge of what he was doing or saying, and with his arms and face working desperately he commenced repeating the word "Bramha, Bramha," perhaps a hundred times, as fast as he could get the word out. It was the vocative of Bramha, the first person of the Hindu Trinity of Bramha, Vishnu, and Siva. Had I needed any further proof of the devilish character of some of these practices in these meetings I had it now to the full (38:93).

Another documented case occurred in Los Angeles. There we read:

A woman got this so-called gift of tongues, and a reputable Chinaman hearing her, said that he understood her quite well—that she spoke his dialect of Chinese. Pressed for an interpretation he declined, saying that the utterance was the vilest of the vile.

In our judgment the facts justify the conclusion that these "signs" are of an unholy spirit of Satan; that he is now producing a poor counterfeit for the deception of a class whom he cannot reach otherwise (38:97).

Surely, even those who will disagree that the modern phenomenon of tongues is demonic in origin would be wise to thoughtfully consider such matters, before attributing the work to the Holy Spirit.

Please keep in mind also that Satan can calmly speak the truth in an understood language. However, this does not mean that it is right for an individual to yield to him. Take, for example, the account in Acts 16:16-18. This girl's vocal chords were being used by Satan to deliver a message. She told everyone, "These men are the servants of the most high God, which shew unto us the way of salvation" (Acts 16:17b). What she said was true and seemed to be a tribute to the evangelists and the Gospel, yet it was evil because of its source. Hence we read, "But

Paul, being grieved, turned and said to the spirit, I command thee in the name of Jesus Christ to come out of her. And he came out the same hour" (Acts 16:18). Paul would not even suffer satanic glossolalia which was true. It was not God honoring, nor could it be, and must be stopped.

Again the danger in the emphasis on this manifestation can be:

3. RELATED TO SUPERSTITION

In both 1 Corinthians 13:2 and 14:2 Paul refers to "mysteries." This is not mere chance, for the backdrop to these chapters is the pagan mystery religions' heathen mosaic. These, complete with the use of ritual gibberish or unintelligible language, emphasized the hidden secrets (mysteries) of the gods which only the initiated could know. Eric Gurr reminds us that:

> We learn from ancient Greece and Rome of certain remarkable people who, under particular stimulants, delivered unintelligible utterances, which afterwards were "interpreted" by "gifted" persons. Virgil (70-19 B.C.) in his celebrated poem, the Aeneid, draws a vivid picture of the ancient pagan prophetess speaking with tongues. He describes the quickly changing color, disheveled hair, panting breast, apparent increase of stature as the "god" draws near, filling the prophetess with what they called the "divine afflatus," when the voice of the medium lost its mortal's ring. Also, Plato attributes a peculiar dialect to the gods, inferring this from dreams and oracles, and especially from demoniacs, "who do not speak their own language or dialect, but that of the demons, who are entered into them (69:4)."

The ecstatic speech of the worshippers also played an important part in these pagan religions. They were regarded as the sign of the god's favor. Each devotee who uttered these "tongues" believed he was in intimate conversational contact with his god. Though the meaning of the words was not known by the worshipper, they were supposedly known by the god or spirit to whom he was praying.

It is against this canvas that the picture in 1 Corinthians chapters 12, 13 and 14 is painted. The same superstition[5] as occurred in the worship of Diana in the pagan temple up on the Acropolis was invading the church. There was a lack of knowledge of God's Word and so there was a subjective interpretation placed upon what was happening. Thus, when they attributed spiritual meaning to ecstatic utterances that had no meaning, they were merely transferring their superstition from the hill to the church.

However there is a need to check the experience by the Word of God. What does the Bible teach about tongues? Have they ceased? This is the application that must be made, rather than the subjective interpretation of an experience which grows from a learned response mechanism. Only a sound knowledge of the Scriptures can keep us from such superstitious interpretations that plummet us back into the Corinthian confusion.

Remember, the Devil is not necessarily an evil looking man in a red suit, having a long tail and carrying a pitchfork in his hand. The Bible tells us, "Satan himself is transformed into an angel of light" (2 Cor. 11:14). Significantly this was originally written to the Corinthian Church which was being deceived by, "false apostles, deceitful workers, transforming themselves into the apostles of Christ" (2 Cor. 11:13). Surely, the wise of today will search the Scriptures to gain a spiritually mature insight into these matters, which will save them from the superstitious gobbledegook, that today passes for a superior Christianity.

We come now to a fourth area of examination concerning the tongues movement, bringing us to the contention that:

---

[5] Superstition: "A belief or notion entertained, regardless of reason or knowledge, of the ominous significance of a particular thing, circumstance, occurrence, proceeding, or the like." (*The American College Dictionary*, ed. C. L. Barnhard, New York: Random House, 1959, page 1216).

D. The Reason is Multiple

In beginning to analyze modern glossolalia, Donald Burdick well states:

> When a person asserts that the New Testament gift of tongues as a normal occurrence ceased at the end of the apostolic age, he is required by that denial to explain the current phenomenon which is being designated as biblical tongues. If the Lord is no longer giving the gift of tongues, what is occurring among Pentecostals and neo-Pentecostals today? One cannot fairly deny the continuation of New Testament glossolalia and yet refuse to face up to the present-day phenomenon (8:59).

Having spoken about the spiritual danger in at least some of the modern phenomena, our attention turns to the many faceted psychological reason for tongues. A variety of writers have made reference to this matter. Let me glean from some of their analyses.

Schofield ties the phenomenon to the same psychological power that produces stigmata when we writes:

> Two things must be understood, first, that the mind extends far beyond the limits of consciousness and that the unconscious part has entire power over the body; not only in causing and curing disease, but in producing under certain conditions, without the knowledge or will of the conscious mind, but chiefly as the result of suggestion—stigmata or wounds and bruises all over the body, sometimes in perfect imitation of the five wounds of our lord, trances, contortions of all sorts under emotion, cries and languages not previously spoken, also mysterious utterances or strange voices, and many other phenomena well known in spiritualistic circles.
>
> The best conditions for producing these natural but rare phenomena are a weakened body, overstrained nerves, the presence of numbers, concentration on the desired signs or gifts, strong suggestions as to possessing them, and powerful influences (38:118).

Because of the possible psychological nature of modern tongues, J.H. Pickford states that:

> Given four or five conditions we can produce or duplicate speaking in tongues. These basic elements enter into the experience. We can only name them; not develop the complications:
>
> a. *Dissatisfaction.* We are disillusioned with ourselves and our accomplishment; we don't seem to be getting anywhere; we are not what we would like to be. We lack something within ourselves.
>
> b. *Excitement.* The emotions are aroused; the feelings are heightened and the thresholds of the rational processes are lowered so that the emotions take control.
>
> c. *Suggestion.* The planting in our consciousness of what we need and how to get it; the letting go and the giving over to an experience we have been structured to receive. We are told how to do it and how to expect it.
>
> d. *Expectation.* The looking for, and reaching after; the expectancy that it is there for us and that we are going to experience it.
>
> e. *Inhibition.* In many cases a person has experienced a great deal of inhibition; there has been a bottling up of the inner yearning that he has found difficult to express or communicate and now, in and through the charismatic experience, the inhibitions are overcome (75:8).

With this George E. Gardiner, himself a former Pentecostal minister, agrees when he writes:

> The desire for experience coupled with instruction, motivation, and the approval of the peer group produces ecstatic speech. I have publicly said many times, "Give me a group of people who will do what I tell them to do; sing, relax, anticipate and go through the right motions and it will be only a matter of time before some will speak ecstatically!" It is a psychological phenomenon and bears no resemblance to the tongues of the Bible (17:53)!

Ira Jay Martin refers to tongues as a "psychic catharsis" brought about by a conflict between maturity and self-fulfillment and the ability to achieve this. (25:50-52).

Now what facets of this psychological reason can be named as contributing to tongues-speaking? First of all, I would suggest:

1. ECSTACY

This can be defined as a highly emotional state. In the cases where tongues are the product of ecstacy the speaker is lifted out of his ordinary frame of mind. Inhibitions are set aside and a kind of psychological delirium is produced. Says Dr. George Cutten:

> In ecstasy there is a condition of emotional exaltation in which the one who experiences it is more or less oblivious of the external world, and loses to some extent his self-consciousness and his power of rational thought and self-control. Some persons seem to have acquired the ability to enter this state voluntarily (11:4).

His definition would fit that of most psychiatrists and psychologists.

Describing the attendant excesses that sometimes accompany this ecstacy, Gordon Brown writes:

> A woman of culture and standing in Scotland, after taking up with Pentecostalism, might be seen preaching on the street with her disheveled hair flowing in the wind. If that be thought unseemly, what shall we say of the other women lying on the floor in a "room 120", and having to be covered with coats, sometimes heavy ones so they will stay on, to preserve a semblance of decency? A student of the Pentecostal Bible School told in a gathering here in Toronto how she got the power in a meeting later to find herself under the keys of the piano, although she never knew how she got there. At one tabernacle I attended, the sounds from the prayer room reminded me of the screams of loons on a wild lake in the dead

of night. The "holy laugh", the baby gibberish, and the general disorder defy description (81:75).

While all do not exhibit these symptoms, they are not uncommon.

Pentecostalist Alice F. Luce describes the throws of the ecstacy as some receive the baptism:

> The shaking, trembling, quivering of the lips or prostration on the ground are most common among those who are receiving the Baptism.... When the Holy Spirit has to shake us violently it is because there is still ... something of the flesh which He desires to shake out of all of us (23:235f).

The high degree of emotionalism is classically presented in her sympathetic description.

Describing how it felt for her personally to have received "the baptism with the Holy Spirit," a Presbyterian woman testified:

> All the joys of my life were blended together in one ecstatic moment—all the fun of childhood, my first date, the moment when the man I wanted asked me to share life with him, the exultation of the finished sex longing ... I had the sensation I was almost floating instead of walking (65:13).

Surely it is not unfair to speak of this in terms of ecstacy!

Ecstacy then is one facet of the psychological reason for tongues-speaking. Another is:

2. SELF-HYPNOSIS

Howard Sugden reveals the following conversation with a Bible teacher of some renown who was formerly involved in the charismatic movement.

> I asked him about it. "Tell me, is it real?" His response was this: "Among the folk that I know who speak in tongues it is ninety percent self-hypnosis. You have to cross a certain line in order to do it. If you don't cross that line it just doesn't happen (60:10)."

Often this is the result of a search after something more satisfying in one's life. It may be preceded by a period of frustration, spiritual anxiety and longing. Then the "Baptism" is presented as the end of the search for joy, satisfaction, spiritual reality and the abundant life.

Usually, the moment that "the gift" is received there are others around to give group approval. There may have been a time of intense spiritual introspection, instruction and prayer. All of these combine to trigger the correct psychological effect in some people.

Describing the atmosphere of large (and we may add small) charismatic gatherings, Schofield says:

> There is much hypnotic power, both conscious and unconscious in large crowds. Slow, monotonous singing while bowed in prayer, with constant repetition greatly favors this.... But, alas, all extremes of excitement and of hypnosis are too easily regarded as sane behavior, and are accepted as of God, provided they occur in connection with religious assemblies (38:120).

Thus, self-hypnosis becomes a part of an individual's experience, producing tongues-speaking. In turn, this is interpreted as normative religious behavior to be repeated often in charismatic worship.

Another part of the psychological reason for tongues might be decribed as an:

3. APHASIC REACTION

An aphasic reaction, in layman's terms, is a kind of mental short circuit. The brain is seen as a master computer in which is stored everything we have ever seen, or heard.[6] Tongues may, therefore, simply be a confused linking of speech syllables which by-pass the conscious mind.

---

[6] Bergsma quotes from an article by Warren S. McCullough entitled "The Brain as a Computing Machine" from *Electric Engineering* June 1949. In this article the brain is regarded as being like a computer able to store facts to be recalled when demanded by the program fed into it. Unlike the machine, the brain has an unlimited capacity for storage of facts. Everything that has entered it is stored there for future recall!

Dr. Stuart Bergsma, a psychiatrist, suggests:

> The speaker takes the shortcut of a reflex action,
> bringing a dissociation upon himself, by which words
> do not go before the rational cerebral cortex for in-
> spection, reflection and judgment as to whether they
> make sense, but are sent out directly via the efferent
> nerves as speech (3:16).

This releases the person from adult inhibitions and
speech controls thus allowing for nonsense syllables,
some foreign terms or even long passages of language
stored in memory.

Dr. E. Mansell Pattison, a member of the Christian
Association for Psychological Studies and currently an
instructor at the University of Washington School of
Medicine, says:

> The product of our analysis is the demonstration of
> the very natural mechanisms that produce
> glossolalia. As a psychological phenomenon,
> glossolalia is easy to produce and readily understan-
> dable.... I can add my own observation from clinical
> experience with neurological and psychiatric pa-
> tients. In certain types of brain disorders resulting
> from strokes, brain tumors, etc., the patient is left
> with disruptions in his automatic physical speech cir-
> cuit patterns. If we study these "aphasic" patients
> we can observe the same decomposition of speech
> that occurs in schizophrenic thought and speech pat-
> terns, which are structurally the same as glossolalia.
> This data can be understood to demonstrate that the
> same stereotypes of speech will result whenever con-
> scious, willful control of speech is interfered with,
> whether by injury to the brain, by psychosis, or by
> passive renunciation of willful control. This cor-
> roborates our previous assessment that glossolalia is
> a stereotyped pattern of unconsciously controlled
> vocal behavior which appears under specific emo-
> tional conditions (73:2).

Thus, Dr. Pattison confirms that an aphasic reaction can
be produced when a person becomes involved in any

emotion which interferes with the conscious control of his brain patterns. However, from a psychiatric point of view, this could be viewed as a disordered mental state not unlike schizophrenic reactions.

Another psychological reason might be:

4. CRYPTOMNESIA

A question might be raised as to how these psychological facets could ever produce speech in a real language apparently unknown to the speaker. I have already referred to the brain in terms of a computer in which all memory is stored. Often this storing is accomplished unconsciously and then forgotten, but under certain conditions can be brought to mind.

Such a phenomenon can apply to language also. In this respect a person retains in his memory speech in a foreign language which, under normal circumstances, cannot be recalled. However, when the necessary psychological trigger is pulled, this stored speech is released and the person speaks fluently in a language he has never learned under normal circumstances. This is similar to Carl G. Jung's idea of "collected unconscious." Morton T. Kelsey explains Jung's position in these words:

> If the Jungian idea of the collective unconscious is accepted, speaking in tongues makes real sense, as a breakthrough into consciousness of a deep level of the collective unconsciousness similar to the dream. Linguistic patterns belonging to the past, to some other part of the present, or to some other level of being take possession of the individual and are expressed by him (20:216-217).

Dr. George Cutten has cited examples of such a phenomenon, also called "exalted memory." He describes the case of an illiterate servant who in a delirium spoke at length in Hebrew, Greek and Latin. Upon investigation it was found that she had served in the home of a clergyman and had heard him recite long passages in these languages (11:176). Apart from demonic interference, this probably is the source of any instance where a foreign language is heard in a tongues gathering. Thus, again the source is psychological rather than spiritual.

One more facet of this psychological reason may simply be:

5. INTENSE EARNESTNESS

By this I mean that it may be the result of an overwhelming longing for a deeper life. Schofield describes these people as:

> Earnest godly people, who are ever eager to hear and to know about the latest sensation in religion, and who, having embraced the higher teaching,... are eager to surrender every faculty they possess, if thereby God may be glorified (38:119).

A more recent writer, Charles Ryrie, adds that in these people, "... all the interest (in tongues) relates to a genuine desire to have a deeper experience with God" (35:167). Thus the very desire of God's people for a more consecrated and dedicated life becomes the occasion for tongues to invade their lives.

In his inimitable way, Ralph L. Keiper, deals with this reason in the following summation:

> Having met some of them and having read much of the literature coming from the tongues movement, I am persuaded that many Episcopalians, Presbyterians, Methodists, Baptists seek this experience for spiritual reality. Sincere students in the university world, especially those who have been assailed by intellectual doubts and have had the Bible questioned by their professors, have experienced an intellectual and emotional vacuum which they long to have filled. For them speaking in tongues has been a genuine religious experience emotionally.
>
> The Episcopal and Presbyterian churches are not known for their spiritual "rowdyism." In fact, they are generally so polite and worship God with such finesse that their emotional life has been religiously starved. Since the "right" people are beginning to

speak in tongues, it is possible for them to have this experience without doing any damage to their social status.

Evangelicals seek this experience as a refuge and a shelter from the internecine warfare which has been waged among them over the most insane things. Becoming exasperatingly exhausted by doctrinal deviltry, they, too, long for a respite from their puny puffings over pigmy problems. Then of course there are those of the orthodox who, on a much higher level because of their intellects, have argued themselves into logic's grave, and by their syllogistic death long to be resurrected from the deadness of their dilemma.

We joined them in looking for a deeper life and a more intense love of the Lord Jesus Christ. We believe, however, that this can only be found in one way: in a daily walk with our Lord, in obedience to the light of His Word (56:21-23).

To this we merely add a hearty, Amen.

To conclude: tongues-speaking is a phenomenon but not an unexplainable one. When one puts together the methodology used to instruct those seeking after it, the analysis of the product produced, the danger of Satanic intrusion, and the multiple psychological reasons for them, he is not surprised at their appearance.

The thing to keep in mind, however, is that the standard for believing, or not believing, in charismatic glossolalia is the Word of God. Bruner is absolutely correct when he states, "The test of anything calling itself Christian is not its significance or its success or its power, though these make the test more imperative. The test is truth" (6:33). Had we no other answer to the tongues phenomenon than the teaching of the Scriptures that they have ceased, that would be enough. The present chapter is merely an attempt to show that, even beyond the teaching of the Scriptures, the modern tongues phenomenon can be shown not to be a replica of Biblical tongues. Do not be misled by the charismatic claims for Biblical tongues-speaking today.

7

THE RELATION OF TONGUES
TO INTERPRETATION

As surely as the supernatural ability from God to speak in a foreign language was a gift of the Holy Spirit, just as surely was "the interpretation of tongues" (1 Cor. 12:10) also a Spiritual gift. In our media-oriented world we have become used to hearing foreign languages translated into English, *simultaneously*. This is particularly evident in programs originating from the United Nations in New York City, or from the Canadian Parliament in Ottawa. As we listen, we marvel that these translators can so readily *interpret* what is being said.

These translations differ from the gift mentioned in 1 Cor. 12:10, in that they take years of language study. Then, there is also much time spent developing the facility to do simultaneous translation. What we hear, therefore, is the fruit of long years of diligent human effort. However, these translations are similar to the gift in one very important point, for they are interpretations of a foreign, translatable language. The individual doing the interpreting in this way becomes the medium through which the speaker addresses the audience.

Now this brings us to the first point that must be made:

A. INTERPRETATION WAS A GIFT

As the tongues, or languages, were not the product of a learning process , so the interpretation was not the product of an acquired knowledge. This ability was a matter of a sovereignly bestowed gift. It was given "by the same Spirit" (1Cor. 12:8-9) as any of the other gifts.

Thus, it was not the fruit of long years of diligent study but rather an instantaneously bestowed ability.

The gift of interpretation was similar to modern translation work, in that its purpose was to transcribe a message from one language to another. The word in 1 Cor. 12:10 is *hermēneia* and is also found in 1 Cor. 14:26. It is a word meaning to explain or interpret and is used for explaining words of different languages (48:167).

Interestingly enough, the word includes the name Hermēs, who in Greek mythology was the son of Jupiter and Maia. Hermēs is the Greek name of the pagan god, Mercury, who was regarded as the messenger and interpreter of the gods (1:167). Thus, the translator was God's Hermēs, who interpreted the message supernaturally given through the gift of tongues.

The word interpret occurs four times in the three gift chapters of Corinthians (1 Cor. 12:30; 14:5, 13, 27). It is the verb *diamēneuō*, which refers generally to the translation of a language and not to the explanation of ecstatic speech. The fact is that with the addition of *dia*, meaning "through," the word is an intensified form of hermēneia. This verb means "to interpret fully" and its noun form (1 Cor. 14:28), therefore, refers to "a thorough interpreter" (48:268).

Writing of diamēneuō, Robert Gundry explains:

> Although the verb might refer to the explaining of mysterious utterances, its usage in biblical Greek militates against this understanding. Out of 21 uses of ermēneuō (apart from the uses in 1 Cor. 12-14) in the LXX and in the New Testament, 18 refer to translation, 2 to explanation, and 1 to satire or a figurative saying (68:300).

There can be little doubt, therefore, that its usage in 1 Corinthians should likewise be seen as the translation of actual languages.

In New Testament usage the gift of interpretation may also have been possessed by the speaker in tongues. The speaker could in that case interpret the message he had just spoken, thus elevating the gift of tongues to a benefit close to prophecy.

> I would that ye all spake with tongues, but rather that ye prophesied: for greater is he that prophesieth than he that speaketh with tongues, except he interpret, that the church may receive edifying (1 Cor. 14:5).

In this case tongues and interpretation would be a hyphenated gift.

Later in the chapter, Paul recommends use of tongues. "Wherefore let him that speaketh in an unknown tongue pray that he may interpret" (1Cor. 14:13). Indeed, it may well be that the gift of interpretation was latent in each person who possessed the gift of tongues. This would explain why the apostle advises praying for a gift that was the sovereign work of the Holy Spirit in its bestowal (1 Cor. 12:11). It would also add further weight to Paul's advocacy of tongues-interpretation as gifts dually used by the same person (1 Cor. 14:5). Whatever the background, it is clear that interpretation was a gift.

We come to a second matter of importance in seeking to understand this gift:

B. INTERPRETATION WAS PRIMARY TO TONGUES

Though apparently the gift of interpretation was not needed outside the church assembly (1 Cor. 14:18-19) as, for example, on Pentecost or where Paul would be doing missionary work among people of other languages, it was needed inside the church. The reason for this is obvious. The church was the mainstream into which the various language tributaries flowed. Thus, for the congregation to understand messages given in a language other than their own, an interpreter was needed.

In view of this cosmopolitan nature of the church, tongues were forbidden unless an interpreter was present. The rule was, "if there be no interpreter, let him keep silence in the church; and let him speak to himself, and to God" (1 Cor. 14:28). Paul had already stated that tongues without interpretation would merely cause outsiders who are "unlearned, or unbelievers," to "say that ye are mad" (1 Cor. 14:23). Primary, therefore, to the use of tongues was the assurance that they would be interpreted so that the others would understand the message.

This, of course, leads us to believe that interpreters were well known in the congregation. They could be identified as present and their presence would allow the gift of tongues to be exercised (1 Cor. 14:28). If, on the other hand, there were no identifiable interpreters present, then tongues were not to be allowed.

Again, in our search of the Scriptures for an understanding of this gift, we find:

C. INTERPRETATION WAS TO BE CONFINED

It would seem that in the Corinthian Church confusion, a number of interpreters would translate the same message. "Everyone of you ... hath an interpretation" (1 Cor. 14:26). The problem was that these interpretations were not always complimentary. Indeed they often conflicted, bringing confusion rather than edification.

For this reason, Paul emphasizes the need for order in the practice of tongues and interpretation. Three times over this is stressed. "Let all things be done unto edifying" (1 Cor. 14:26). "For God is not the author of confusion, but of peace, as in all churches of the saints" (1 Cor. 14:33). "Let all things be done decently and in order" (1 Cor. 14:40). The greatest need of the Church at Corinth was order and decency.

In order to bring about some sanity to the situation, Paul set down these simple rules, "If any man speak in an unknown tongue, let it be by two, or at the most by three, and that by course; and let one interpret" (1 Cor. 14:27). Only a total sequence of three manifestations of tongues were to be allowed in any single service. Then only one person was to interpret, after the three speakers had taken their turn. In this way there was no possibility of conflict, or confusion, for the trumpet would not be blowing an uncertain sound (1 Cor. 14:8-9).

By the way, this indicates that the gift of interpretation was "multi-lingual" in application. There was not merely the ability to translate a single language but, as the tongues were of "divers kinds," so also the interpreter was equipped to meet the diverse challenge. The interpreter could, therefore, translate for the three speakers without any difficulty.

One final important matter rewards our search for a Biblical understanding of this gift.

D. INTERPRETATION WAS FOR EDIFICATION

Actually the overriding rule of chapters 12, 13 and 14 of 1 Corinthians is that all done must edify the body. In this respect, Paul reserves some of his harshest criticism for those who were selfishly employing tongues with disregard for interpretation. Only if tongues were interpreted did they have any profit in the church.

Listen to Paul's statements, "For he that speaketh in an unknown tongue speaketh not unto men, but unto God" (1 Cor. 14:2). "He that speaketh in an unknown tongue edifieth himself" (1 Cor. 14:4). "For if I pray in an unknown tongue, my spirit prayeth, but my understanding is unfruitful" (1 Cor. 14:14). "I thank my God, I speak with tongues more than ye all: Yet in the church I had rather speak five words with my understanding, that by my voice I might teach others also, than ten thousand words in an unknown tongue" (1 Cor. 14:18-19). It was dreadfully easy for those with the gift of tongues to selfishly misuse it to gratify self. Thus, the purpose of edification of the church was lost.

This is also the contrast between tongues and prophecy in 1 Cor. 14:23-25. Tongues without interpretation appeared as madness to outsiders, but an understandable prophetic utterance convinced sinners. Without interpretation, tongues did not glorify God or help other people.

You can see, then, that this gift of interpretation was of utmost importance. Any who were spiritual at all would seek to "excel to the edifying of the church" (1 Cor. 14:12) says Paul. Then he adds, "Wherefore let him that speaketh in an unknown tongue pray that he may interpret" (1 Cor. 14:13). That which salvaged tongues and elevated it to a gift which was useful to edify the church, was the gift of interpretation.

Of course, without the gift of tongues the raison d'etre for interpretation was gone. The only message an interpretation had was that of the speaker being translated. Thus, when tongues ceased, so did interpretation. This gift too was temporary and we do well not to be misled by the messages which pour forth from its supposed "use" today.

8

THE RECORD OF TONGUES
IS PERILOUS HISTORY

The pearls of wisdom which drop from the lips of the subjective charismatic exponents, can lead to dire peril for their misled followers. History records, and present day happenings concur, that those involved, in seeking to restore what the Scriptures teach have ceased, leave themselves open to psychic and Satanic perils. We do well, therefore, to ponder thoughtfully at this point some historic lessons on the subject.

First of all, the charismatic phenomenon historically has:

A. THE PERIL OF EXTRA-BIBLICAL REVELATION

By this I mean that one can find similar outbreaks of charismatic phenomena in centuries gone by. These invariably leaned heavily toward extra-Biblical revelation. What we are seeing in this century is by no means new and neither is the opposition to it by thoughtful students of God's Word.

As far back as 150 A.D., an outbreak of charismatic phenomena swept the religious world. It arose under the teaching of Montanus, "a man of extravagant opinion and ascetic rigor" (10:18). Eusebius, a fourth-century historian, tells us that he was possessed of a spirit which made him rave in a kind of ecstatic trance and babble in a jargon similar to what is called tongues in our day. He claimed to be a prophet and, together with two prophetesses named Maximilla and Priscilla, who had deserted their husbands to follow him, he began his "ministry" in the region of Phrygia. Adds Criswell:

Remember, this occurred in about A.D. 150. Polycarp, the disciple of the Apostle John, was still alive and was pastor at Smyrna. Papias, the disciple of John, was still alive and pastor at Hierapolis. Even in their days, the days of the disciples of the apostles, the history books say that the phenomenal, supernatural gifts of the apostles ceased to exist (10:18).

Montanus claimed for himself and his two prophetesses the supernatural powers and gifts of the apostles and prophets. His work was characterized by ecstasies and utterances which added to the Holy Scriptures. He claimed that "as the writings of Paul superseded those of Moses; so his ecstasies and utterances were to supersede those of Paul" (10:18). Indeed, according to Hippolytus who wrote in the third century, the followers of Montanus began to magnify these women above the Apostles and in some instances claimed that there was something more in them than in Christ. So strong was this movement, that such a man as Tertulian was caught up in it. He writes concerning the so-called gifts of revelations and ecstatic visions in the Spirit which these prophetesses claimed to have and which were received as such among the churches.

However out of this came a tremendous controversy. The debate raged over whether his trances, visions, prophecies and gifts were real or counterfeit. Were the extraordinary powers of the apostles to continue in the church, or had they ceased to exist? Out of this great controversy came two decisive conclusions by men of God who based their findings on the Word of God. First, that the Bible is complete and the canon of the Holy Scriptures is closed. Secondly, that no man—Montanus included—could claim extra-Biblical revelation by ecstatic utterance, or by prophetic declaration, or by any other extraordinary means.

All of this, of course, is in keeping with the teaching of the Word of God. Rev. 22:18-19 is clear and definite:

If any man shall add unto these things, God shall add unto him the plagues that are written in this book:

> And if any man shall take away from the word of the book of this prophecy, God shall take away his part out of the book of life, and out of the holy city, and from the things which are written in this book.

No prophecy, no vision, no ecstatic utterance can give a word from heaven that is not already in the Word of God.

Again all the miraculous avowals that were made on the basis of apostolic gifts, the churches rejected. Criswell says that:

> Montanus claimed that the early sign-gifts were to continue forever. The churches answered that miraculous gifts were never promised the church as a personal inheritance. After the closing of the canon, and after the death of the apostles, those marvelous powers such as the ability to raise the dead ceased. The work of the Holy Spirit became primarily the work of illuminating the Word of God, regenerating the soul, and forming the life and mind of Christ in the heart of the individual believer. Thus spoke the churches in the conflict that arose over Montanus (10:19).

But some might say, "Surely if we can show some great authenticating sign, people will more readily believe!" Such a statement, though given by sincere believers in our Lord Jesus Christ, is spawned in hell. It mimics the statement of Dives to Abraham in Luke 16 which records their conversation about the rich man's five brothers. There he states that the Word of God is not sufficient to produce belief, "but if one went unto them from the dead, they will repent" (Luke 16:30). This claim is still answered clearly, definitely and irrevocably by heaven in the words, "If they hear not Moses and the prophets, neither will they be persuaded, though one rose from the dead" (Luke 16:31).

Only "an evil and adulterous generation seeketh after a sign" (Matt. 12:39). That is why such a generation can be deceived by Satan's wonders. It is also the reason that we read concerning "that wicked one" of 2 Thessalonians 2, that his:

> coming is after the work of Satan with all power and
> signs and lying wonders,
> And with all deceivableness of unrighteousness in
> them that perish; because they received not the love
> of the truth, that they might be saved (2 Thess.
> 2:9-10).

Submission to the authority of the completed and final
Word of God is the only means of maintaining one's
spiritual equilibrium in this present evil world.

To all intents and purposes, the Montanism controversy should have ended the charismatic controversy.
However, it did not. Perilous outbreaks of ecstasies and
related extra-Biblical phenomena have occurred from
time to time throughout history. Today's outbreak is no
exception and no different.

There is a second danger in the charismatic phenomenon as seen historically, that is:

B. The Peril of Carnal Excess

Of course, excess was the key word at Corinth. They
were well used to the excesses of heathen idolatry. When
they were saved and joined the church some of those excesses were "sanctified" and brought over with the converts. All kinds of excesses were, therefore, invading the
church.

We do well to remind ourselves of the background
against which the Epistle in general and chapters 12 to
14 in particular were written. Bryant does this well in
the following description:

> At Corinth was found one of the centers of worship
> for the ancient mystery religions. Those religions
> were like Canaanite religion in the sense that they
> worshipped fertility and the cycles of nature. High
> on one of the Corinthian hills stood Acrocorinthus, a
> magnificant acropolis, with a temple to Aphrodite,
> the Greek fertility goddess of love. The temple was
> filled with priestesses who were little more than
> prostitutes. The ritual of worship involved sexual
> orgies. Frenzied rituals indicated that the priestesses
> were ready for the men of Corinth to come up to the

temple for these orgies. During these rituals the priestesses would lose emotional control of themselves and would break out into ecstatic utterances, or unknown tongues. No doubt some of these priestesses were converted under Paul's preaching. Out of their religion they brought over into their Christian experience the only religious expression which was not immoral in itself, the practice of those frenzied, ecstatic utterances. They simply made those utterances in the worship of Jesus instead of in the worship of Aphrodite (7:73).

Such an understanding should make us wary of desiring to pattern our church life after the like of the members in Corinth. Surely, we would be better to pattern ourselves after the teaching the Apostle gives to correct such excess. But pattern their lives after that excess, people do, as their perilous history records.

A. T. Schofield, M.D., in his book *Christian Sanity* outlines some of these:

In 1374 there was a dreadful religious dancing mania which began in Aix. There were hundreds of dancing men and women screaming and foaming at the mouth, and all this coupled with wonderful visions of Christ and the Saints. There were many cases of recovery of sight to the blind. This mania spread all over that part of Germany like wild fire, and yet there can be no doubt that multitudes carried away by it were earnest and true Christians.

In Italy, at another time, thousands of people were suddenly affected with the literal "fear" of God; and persons of noble and ignoble birth, men and women and even children five years old, walked naked in public two and two, each with a scourge of leather thongs, and lashed themselves on their bare backs, with tears and blood accompanying the act. There were many thousands thus all over Italy crying to God for mercy.

In 1707 and following years London was disturbed by a noisy group of French and English fanatics, who combined the highest religious pretensions and the most Scriptural language with prophecies, speaking in tongues which were accompanied by all sorts of contortions and by many immoralities. The movement began by three French Protestant refugees coming over in the reign of Queen Anne; and amongst their followers were Sir Richard Bulkeley a wealthy baronet, a prebendary of Salisbury Cathedral, several physicians, a learned scientist, the tutor of the Duke of Bedford, Lady Jane Forbes, and many others. These do not seem to have been deceivers, but earnest Christian men deceived and deluded by lying spirits, which they firmly believed were the Holy Spirit of God (38:76, 77).

Such excesses are not typical of all charismatic phenomena, I am sure, but the fertility of the extra-Biblical ground in which they grow is a common denominator throughout their perilous history.

Perhaps no section of history is clearer on this than that revealing:

C. THE PERIL OF PENTECOSTAL ROOTS

What are the historical roots of modern Pentecostalism? The movement has gained such acceptance, that it is hard to believe that it was not here a century ago! Perhaps those who join the group today are unaware of these foundations.

W. Gordon Brown, former Dean of Central Baptist Seminary in Toronto, writes:

But the movement most like the Pentecostalism of this century was led by Edward Irving. When this Scotsman left the Presbyterian Church, many went with him, and began a church of their own to "demonstrate a higher style of Christianity". For a time his following was large; but when meetings became very disorderly, people were repelled. Speaking in tongues appeared in an obscure part of Scotland in 1828 with Mary Campbell, a cripple, who heard from neighbors that they had the "gift".

Gradually tongues came to the Irvingites about three years later. The tongues, the message apparently in interpretation, the exhaustion which followed,—these and other phenomena closely resemble those found in the modern movement. Prominent Irvingites claims are certainly in line with those we shall find in Pentecostalism; harmony of practice with the primitive church, a work greater than the reformation, restoration of the gifts in these last days, this restoration a "warning cry" to prepare for the second coming, prophecy in interpretation of Scripture. Irving himself held "the idea that disease was a sin, and that no man with faith in the Lord ought to be overpowered by it". We think it also significant that Irving called his movement the "Latter Rain"; said he: "This outpouring of the Spirit is known in the Scriptures as the 'Latter Rain', of which I deem the present religious revivals of the last thirty years to be the first droppings of the shower" (81:14).

There can be no doubt that Irving is the source of much of today's Pentecostal interpretation of faith and practice. In many ways these roots remind us of the heresies of the Montanists, rejected so decisively by the early church.

In his book, Schofield analyzes the beginnings of the so-called Irvingite Movement which really began, via Pentecostalism, the charismatic controversy we face today. A document by one of Irving's disciples, a Mr. Robert Baxter, is given in full. The writer, a "somewhat heavy Scotch lawyer, of considerable eminence in London at the Parliamentary bar, ... singularly clear, level-headed, and reliable in every way" (38:77), tells of his involvement in the charismatic phenomena of the day.

Because of a lack of understanding of the Scriptures on the matter, he began to (as he thought) "covet earnestly the best gifts." For those he greatly longed, agonized and prayed. Finally he tells us:

In the midst of a prayer-meeting for the first time I was myself seized upon by the power, and in much struggling against it was made to cry out (in a loud and commanding voice) and myself give forth a confession of sin, a prophecy that the messengers of the Lord would go forth and publish to the ends.... the near coming of the Lord Jesus.

I was overwhelmed by this occurrence. I was distinctly conscious of a power acting in me.

In private prayer one day I was much distressed at my wandering thoughts, when suddenly the power came down upon me, and I found myself lifted up in soul to God, my thoughts were riveted, and calmness of mind given me.

By a constraint I cannot describe, I was made to speak, at the same time shrinking from utterance. The utterance was a prayer that the Lord would bestow on me the gifts of His Spirit, the gift of miracles, the gifts of healing, of prophecy, of tongues, and that he would open my mouth to declare His glory. This prayer was forced from me by the constraint of the power which acted upon me: and the utterance was so loud that I put my handkerchief to my mouth to stop the sound that I might not alarm the house. When I had reached the last word the power died off me, and left me filled with amazement, and with a strong conviction, "This is the Spirit of God."

I must testify that looking back upon all that is past (now I know it is of the devil) whenever the power rested on me, I seemed to have joy and peace in the Holy Ghost, and I cannot even now, by feeling alone, discern that it was not really such!

At a meeting while the pastor was speaking the power fell upon me and I was made to speak (in a loud voice), and for two hours or upwards I gave forth prophecies concerning the church; declaring its present state and coming glory, and the return of the Lord. I had no excitement; to myself it was calmness and peace. The words flashed into my mind without forethought, without expectation, without any plan or arrangement; all was the work of the moment, and

I was as the passive instrument of the power which used me.

Mr. Irving said he had doubts as to allowing me to speak in his church; and the power came on me, rebuking him, and reasoning with him, until he sat down and said he did not know what to do. Then the power came on Miss H., who said he must not forbid my speaking. This satisfied him and he yielded at once (38:78).

Remember, this is a lawyer writing. He is a sincere believer in the Lord Jesus Christ. His greatest desire is to glorify God. So, as he put it:

The mistake is awful, if a seducing spirit is entertained as the Holy Spirit. The more devoted the Christian seduced, the more implicit the obedience; and unless God graciously interpose, there can be no deliverance (38:80).

Such, I firmly believe, is the reason for many good people being ensnared by the phenomenon of today's charismatic movement.

But this Scottish lawyer has not finished yet. He goes on to say:

About this time was consummated the masterpiece of doctrinal delusion in the development of the "baptism of fire" as it was thenceforth expounded by me. It was declared "in utterance" that the Lord would again send apostles, by the laying on of whose hands should follow the baptism of fire, which should subdue the flesh, and burn out sin, and give to the disciples of Christ the full freedom of the Holy Ghost, and final victory over the world.

The simultaneous action of the power upon two or more continually occurred, leading them to utter the same words.

In the midst of minds duly prepared, Satan can gradually develop the subjects of his delusion; and going on step by step, can unwarily lead his victims into extravagancies, first by doctrine and next by conduct, which they would, without such gradual preparation, shudder to contemplate.

Some amongst us were found to be speaking by an 'evil spirit' and Mrs. C. and Mrs. E. C. had been much in power to declare it. This troubled me greatly, for I had been led in power to declare the call of one of them to the spiritual ministry.

I treated, however, any doubt as a temptation, I rested implicitly upon the text, "every spirit that confesseth Jesus Christ is come in the flesh is of God," and felt assured that no spirit making that confession could be of Satan. I had heard the confession made several times by the spirit which spoke in myself and others. I ought to have seen that the mere confession in words is not of itself a proof of the spirit being of God, and searched out more fully whether the spirit did really set forth the truth (38:81).

Remember, we are getting an "eye witness account" of the beginnings of Pentecostalism from one who was obviously deeply involved. He is no outsider looking in without any real understanding of the movement. His account is a first hand experience of those early days of the movement.

Perhaps the most devasting revelation Baxter makes concerning the movement comes when he learned Irving's true doctrine concerning our Lord Jesus Christ. Let him tell the story:

At this time Mr. Irving's views became known that the law of the flesh and the law of sin was in Jesus, and only kept down by the Holy Spirit. In April, 1832, Mr. Irving wrote to me: "I believe the flesh of Christ to have been no better than other flesh; but he received such a measure of the Holy Spirit as sufficed to resist its own proclivity to the world and to Satan!"

I then called on Mr. Irving and told him my conviction that we had all been speaking by a lying spirit and not the Spirit of the Lord (38:82).

Much more detail is given, including testimony by others involved, but surely this is sufficient to show that, at the very foundations of the movement, people were perilously deceived by Satan and were also being deceived by wrong doctrine (2 Tim. 3:13).

From the Irvingite beginnings, the movement spread worldwide. Brown traces the roots of that sprawling history.

Modern Pentecostalism is traced to a sort of Bible school in Topeka, Kansas, where, on January 1st, 1901, Mrs. LaBerge, after studying the baptism in the Holy Ghost and praying much in an upper room, asked that hands might be laid upon her head that she might "receive the gift of the Holy Ghost". "It was as hands were laid upon my head that the Holy Spirit fell upon me and I began to speak in tongues, glorifying God. I talked several languages, and it was clearly manifest when a new dialect was spoken."

The tongues-movement spread south from Kansas. A Georgia negro Holiness preacher, W. J. Seymour, and a negress cook carried the message to Los Angeles. There a tenement meeting hall on Azusa Street became the center where, in 1906, many sought "the baptism". On learning that the black brother usually presided at these meetings sitting behind two empty shoe boxes, his head usually in the top one, wearing no necktie as he claimed it choked the glory, those who know anything of the religious excitement found in old revival meetings of southern negroes, will be prepared for the wildest extravagances.

In the fall of that year Sister Mabel Smith and others preached Pentecostalism in Chicago, often speaking in tongues. Thence the message spread over neighboring states. In the same year many "received the baptism" in a mission in Toronto, Canada. Of Mrs. Hebden, a leading figure in the mission, a friend wrote about that time: "Now the Holy Spirit speaks and prays in a tongue through her, and sings, and writes and makes sketches which are like landscapes. Paul exhorts, 'Let him pray that he may interpret.' She has prayed and now interprets. One of the sketches was as clouds rolling up from the earth. Two days after this was given, it was interpreted to her to mean the resurrection of the saints. I heard Mrs. Hebden speak yesterday, writing what she said. It was this, 'God's people should pray for more humility'." Pastor R. E. McAlister, former General Secretary-Treasurer of the Pentecostal Assemblies of Canada, went all the way to Los Angeles to "seek the baptism", and returned to spread the new doctrine. Soon the movement reached London, England, where Mrs. Catherine S. Price was the first to receive "the Pentecostal experience." In 1907 a Pentecostal revival swept Scotland. From London it spread to Norway, Denmark, Sweden, Holland, Russia and Germany. Of the last it could be said in 1912 that "the whole country is honeycombed with Pentecostal missions and assemblies." Pentecostalism also spread to the East in China and India; to the South, in Central and South America; to Egypt, Liberia, Central and South Africa; to New Zealand and Australia. Thus it became a world fellowship within twenty-five years (81:16-18).

Such are the perilous roots of the movement's beginning. Montanus marches again!

This brings us in the fourth place to a consideration of current history and of:

D. THE PERIL OF CHARISMATIC SALESMANSHIP

The roots from which the charismatic movement evolve are clear. Russell T. Hitt, a dissenter who is obviously sympathetic to the movement, writes:

Neo-Pentecostalism has been heralded as a "spontaneous movement of the Spirit of God." But it is not as spontaneous as it may appear. It can be very directly traced to the older Pentecostalism. My friend of many years, the Rev. David Du Plessis, has pioneered and promoted ecumenical Pentecostalism.

The Full Gospel Christian Businessmen's Committee has publicized widely the non-Pentecostal ministers and laymen who have come into the "baptism." The most polished of public relations techniques have been enrolled to advance the movement. While there is certainly nothing wrong with using modern techniques, the neo-Pentecostalism cannot claim complete spontaneity (55:8).

His final statement is as important as his argument for it clearly charges that the movement is man-inspired, if not man-made! Being "experience" oriented, the charismatic movement lends itself well to electronic showmanship. Thus, we have the rise of such programs as "the 700 Club" and "P.T.L." in the States, and "100 Huntley Street" in Canada.

Always there is a smiling Johnny Carson style host. Audiences are encouraged to applaud enthusiastically. Phone banks are revealed as "manned" and the viewers urged to phone in prayer requests, or for counselling, or to tell of some miracle God has done in their lives. The guests are as varied (denominationally) and as prominent (show biz types, sports celebrities, doctors, lawyers, etc.) as possible. Music compliments a cross-section of taste and is mostly subjective in content. Everything is joyful, intense, emotional and studiously childlike. And it works!

The question is, "Is it spontaneous?" Is it a movement of God's spirit, or of man's production and organizational genius? We believe it is the latter and we believe it because of the Bible's teaching concerning the gifts of the spirit. It is perilously close to (if not outright) blasphemy to use "modern technique" to proclaim the existence of that which the Spirit of God teaches through the Word of God has ceased.

In living rooms of many homes sit confused people. Via the electronic media a slick advertising campaign bombards these people daily with the subjective gospel of the charismatic movement. It looks and sounds so exciting and, by contrast, their lives are so mundane and humdrum. Can it not possibly be that such marvelous experiences are for them also? So the gullible—those who do not know the objective truth on these issues as presented in the Word of God—are sucked in. And then, because as we have already seen it is psychologically possible to duplicate the "experience" in their own lives, they are confirmed in their misled understanding.

What has been said about the electronic wizardry of the "big time" exponents of the movement can also be said about the "conferences"—large and small—held around the world. Add to this the small subjective Bible study group method used—often by those who have "a zeal of God, but not according to knowledge" (Rom. 10:2),—and the movement's perils grow.

Is it any wonder, then, that "old time" Pentecostals themselves are unsure of the movement. As Hitt puts it:

> The older Pentecostals have mixed emotions about the phenomenon. They rejoice that believers in the major denominations are receiving the baptism of the Spirit, but they can't understand the non-legalistic behavior of some of the new converts who have not yet learned that Pentecostals don't play bridge, go to the theatre, drink cocktails, smoke cigarettes, and wear so much lipstick (55:8)

Surely a lack of practical life changing power does not represent the work of the Holy Spirit!

In conclusion, before one joins the self-adulation of the charismatic movement he should consider well the course he takes. Extra-Biblical revelation, carnal excess, Irvingite roots and Madison Avenue technique (professional, or learned by osmosis) all combine to make the pathway perilous. How much better to follow the Psalmist's methodolgy when he said, "Thy word is a lamp unto my feet, and a light unto my path" (Psalm 119:105). Then a pilgrim can be sure when he hears the invitation, "This is the way, walk ye in it" (Isa. 30:21), that it is from God. On this basis he will constantly be able to testify truthfully, "I being in the way, the Lord led me" (Gen. 24:27). May it be so for increasing multitudes, O Lord, for Thy dear Name's sake!

9

THE RESULT OF TONGUES IS COUNTERFEIT UNITY

If unity of the body of Christ was of sufficient importance to our Lord that His great high-priestly prayer of John 17 several times records the request "That they all may be one" (John 17:21-22), surely this ought to be of concern to every believer. Further, if one of the objectives of the gifts of the Spirit is that "we all come in the unity of the faith" (Eph. 4:13), then we should also have this as an objective in our lives. We should be, "Endeavoring to keep the unity of the Spirit in the bond of peace" (Eph. 4:3). True unity is a precious thing amongst all true believers.

A. THREE STRIKES AND YOU ARE OUT

But having said that, there is a counterfeit unity as well as true unity. True unity is always objective and has at least three golden links in its harmony. Christ is its center, the Bible is its ground, and the Spirit is its bond. Break the chain at any link and you have mistaken true unity.

What kind of union does the charismatic movement produce? It is one which replaces Christ with an emphasis on the Holy Spirit. Of the work of the Spirit, our Lord said, "He shall not speak of Himself" (John 16:13), "He shall glorify me" (John 16:14). As Victor Matthews states so well:

> He shall not speak of Himself ... This means that the Holy Spirit will not draw attention to Himself. This profound statement, expressed so simply, indicates that the entire ministry of the Spirit is away from

Himself. All endeavors, whether by the individual Christian or by a church or denomination, to place the Holy Spirit at the center of their attention and instruction is, therefore, under divine censure (27:99, 100).

Thus, any movement, which places the emphasis on the Holy Spirit, is differing from the teaching of the doctrine of Christ (2 John 9).

Again the oneness of the movement is on the ground of experience. If one has experienced "the baptism with the Holy Spirit," then he is a fellow traveller. It does not matter what other doctrines he might hold, the experience is the thing. But the Scriptures state, "To the law and to the testimony: if they speak not according to this word, it is because there is no light in them" (Isa. 8:20). How then can one ever hope for Biblical unity when a movement has a oneness of "non-truth?"

The third link in the chain of unity centers in the Holy Spirit. Surely here at least charismatics can know real unity. Wrong again, for the vehicle through which the Holy Spirit speaks is the Word of God. He is the inspirer of the Bible. The Scriptures are His product of inspiration. To set aside the written Word to claim some other "word" of revelation is to belittle the very Spirit one eulogizes.

B. AWAY OUT IN LEFT FIELD

When one understands this, he sees that it is no great wonder that the charismatic movement makes strange bed-fellows. Earle E. Matteson traces the rise of the ecumenical movement from the old liberalism to the new Pentecostalism. In doing so he claims that it was a direct self-serving move on the part of ecumenists that brought Pentecostals into the mainstream of the movement. He goes on to say:

> In their efforts they began to see that their emphasis on the work of the Holy Spirit could fill a vacuum for unsuspecting people. If souls could be won collectively, why could not this new experience be shared

ecumenically? Organizations of business men were developed for this specific purpose. Thus we began to read about a Spirit-filled Baptist, a Spirit-filled Methodist, a Spirit-filled Lutheran, and so on. Through this means the Holy Spirit emphasis became a part of the ecumenical stream (26:119).

How has this move affected the religious scene? Tremendously! Denominational barriers began to fall. Speaking with tongues became the experience of Episcopalians, Orthodox, Presbyterians, Baptist, Lutherans—indeed it would seem that no segment of the church escaped the Pentecostal invasion. As John L. Sherrill put it, "The walls came tumbling down (40:51)."

> This interdenominational phase of the movement became known as the neo-Pentecostal, or charismatic, movement. It was no longer a separate denomination but an experience that transcended all denominational boundary lines. Those sharing the experience in different denominations saw themselves as having more in common with each other than with non-charismatics of the same church. Many confidently predicted that this was the beginning of the greatest revival the world had ever known (64:27).

A new ecumenism had been born.

Commenting on this, Robert Brinsmead speaks of some firsthand contacts with those who are a part of the movement. Out of these come the following very revealing illustrations of this new ecumenism.

> When the neo-Pentecostal movement was getting under way in the Los Angeles area in the early 1960's, I talked to an Assembly of God preacher about the phenomenon. He said. "We used to be the leaders in experiencing the baptism in the Holy Spirit, but not since the Spirit has visited the great historic and Protestant churches. I know an Episcopalian priest in this city who is so liberal he neither believes in the virgin birth nor the resurrection. Yet he has recently received the baptism in the Spirit and

exhibits a marvelous power in his ministry." The Pentecostal preacher shrugged his shoulders and added, "I can't understand why God would give all that power to a fellow so far out on the liberal left."

A few months ago a group of Pentecostal Christadelphians invited me to talk to them. Christadelphians not only deny the divinity of Jesus Christ, but also his pre-existence before His birth in Bethlehem. They also deny the personality of the Holy Spirit. Yet here were a group of Christadelphians who claimed the baptism in the Holy Spirit and spoke with tongues (65:10).

These instances can be multiplied but are sufficient to describe for us the kind of unity being produced. It does not really matter where a person stands in the theological spectrum as long as he has "the baptism of the Holy Spirit." And this experience seems to be available to anyone regardless of how heretical his view!

In view of this, one wonders at the depth of spiritual perception in "evangelical" scholars, such as Clark H. Pinnock of Canada's McMaster Divinity College, when he writes:

> The new Pentecostal movement seems to this observer to be a genuine movement of the Spirit of God renewing His church.... It thrills my soul to see multitudes of people allowing the Spirit to operate freely in their midst (65:13).

Surely he does not rejoice in such old-line, dressed-up liberal ecumenism—or does he?

C. NOT EVEN IN THE BALL PARK

Another sweep of the new ecumenism has brought it into Roman Catholic circles. This caused Presbyterian Robert Witaker to declare enthusiatically, "Catholics have brought a depth and a breadth and a sanity which have saved this movement" (65:13). There had been much flirting with the movement by a variety of the Roman Catholic hierarchy. However with one sudden gesture, Rome dramatically opened her arms and "took in" the charismatic movement.

On Whit Monday 1975 Pope Paul greeted 10,000 cheering charismatics in St. Peter's. Reporting the event, one writer said:

> The high-water mark of the controversial movement was manifested during Pentecost weekend last month when Pope Paul VI unofficially—but unmistakably—conferred his blessing on a historic gathering of Catholic charismatics.
>
> "You have to live in the Spirit," the Pontiff told some 10,000 delegates to the third International Conference on the Charismatic Renewal attending a mass at the high altar of St. Peter's. "The church and the world need what you have—your new joy and enthusiasm. Now go and give it to them (66:45)."

A new respectability now garbed the ecumenical charismatic "advance."

Two "Protestant" observers were in Rome for the memorable occasion. One was J. Rodman Williams, president of Melodyland School of Theology, Anaheim, California, and the other was Louis P. Sheldon, administrator of this same charismatic school. Reporting on the events, they pointed to "four major historic precedents" that occurred at the Rome conference:

> —Cardinal Josef Suenens, primate of Belgium and the ranking Catholic exponent of the charismatic renewal, received special permission from the Pope to celebrate the Eucharist on the high altar of St. Peter's Basilica on May 19, the day after Pentecost. He was assisted by 12 "spirit-filled" bishops and about 400 priests in what apparently was the first specifically charismatic service ever held in St. Peter's.
>
> —There was strong emphasis on lay involvement: "Lay people read Scripture, gave prayers and brought forth a word of prophecy from a select group of 70 prophets and prophetesses who had been spiritually approved by the conference coordinating

committee," Mr. Sheldon said. Twelve lay persons also took an active part in the celebration of the Eucharist.

—Women spoke, read Scripture and prophesied from the Pope's altar, said to be unprecedented.

—During the pontifical Mass on Pentecost and the one the following day, the sound of tongues-speaking and "singing in the Spirit" filled the massive nave of the ancient church—also, it is believed, for the first time (66:45).

Emphasizing the surprise "main event," Readers' Digest reported:

Startling Vatican officials, he permitted Cardinal Suenens, Archbishop of Malines-Brussels in Belgium and a noted charismatic leader, to celebrate Mass from St. Peter's Central Altar, normally reserved for the Pope himself (72:3).

To most Protestants this meant little, but to the Roman Catholic world it was astounding!

Yet we need to be aware that a number of Catholic theologians have stated that the Roman Catholic Church and the charismatic movement are not far apart in theology. You see the position taken by both regarding the Scriptures is remarkably similar. Both hold to only qualified inerrancy and authority concerning the Scriptures since by their doctrines fresh revelation can be given beyond the Biblical Canon. This is true regardless of the protests made to the contrary on the issue by sincere charismatics.

One writer states that to understand the Roman Catholic position on this one needs to:

... study the influence of the nineteenth century John Henry Newman in Vatican II's approach to the Bible and revelation. We can only state the crux of his view here: Newman believed that the Scriptures have reduced only a part of special revelation to written form. There is also revelation which is not found in the Scriptures—a nonpropositional revelation. The mind enables the Christian to come to grips with the written revelation, whereas "intuition" (also called "insight") allows access to unscripturated revelation. The revelation grasped by intuition "fills the gaps and puts flesh on the ribs of that which has been committed to writing (74:19)."

Thus, tradition is held to be of equal value with the Bible, and the Popes can speak infallibly on matters of doctrine giving new revelation from God extending beyond the Canon of Scripture.

On the other hand, charismatics in reality hold the same doctrine. If prophecy, tongues and knowledge have not ceased, then of necessity one must leave room for "inspired utterances" which come from the same source as the Scriptures (i.e. the Holy Spirit), but which are beyond that contained in the Scriptures. Whether or not one claims that they are complimentary and not contrary to the Bible is of little consequence. They are extra-Biblical and, because of their implied source, they must be equally authoritative with the Scriptures.

It is little wonder, then, that Roman Catholic theologian and Benedictine monk, Father Edward O'Connor of Notre Dame can write:

Although they derive from Protestant backgrounds, the Pentecostal churches are not typically Protestant in their beliefs, attitudes or practices (31:23).
... it cannot be assumed that the Pentecostal movement represents an incursion of Protestant influence (31:32).
... Catholics who have accepted Pentecostal spirituality have found it to be fully in harmony with their traditional faith and life. They experience it, not as a borrowing from an alien religion, but as a connatural development of their own (31:28).
... the spiritual experience of those who have been touched by the grace of the Holy Spirit in the Pentecostal movement is in profound harmony with the classical spiritual theology of the Church (31:183).

> ... the experience of the Pentecostal movement tends
> to confirm the validity and relevance of our authentic
> spiritual traditions (31:191).
>
> Moreover, the doctrine that is developing in the
> Pentecostal churches today seems to be going
> through stages very similar to those which occurred
> in the early Middle Ages when the classical doctrine
> was taking shape (31:193, 194).

It is clear that the charismatic movement is, therefore,
doing nothing to unsettle the faith of Catholics, or to
change their traditions either.

O'Connor writes in another book on this very fact,
when referring to Roman Catholics who have become
charismatic:

> Similarly, the traditional devotions of the Church
> have taken on more meaning. Some people have been
> brought back to a frequent use of the sacrament of
> Penance through the experience of the baptism in the
> Spirit. Others have discovered a place for devotion to
> Mary in their lives, whereas previously they had been
> indifferent or even antipathetic toward her. One of
> the most striking effects of the Holy Spirit's action
> had been to stir up devotion to the Real Presence in
> the Eucharist (30:14, 15).

The ecumenical pathway shows both movements leading
to essentially the same place doctrinally.

D. A New Game is Called

But who is receiving whom in this enlarged
charismatic ecumenism? Most astute observers would
agree that the present situation is a little like the old
adage, "Come into my parlor, said the spider to the fly!"
To the Roman Catholic hierarchy, the Protestant charismatics are but separated brethren who need to return to
Mother Church. To many leaders in the charismatic
movement, this might not be a bad idea!

Take, for example, these statements by "Protestant"
theologians on the future of the charismatic movement
in relation to Roman Catholicism. John A. Mackay,

former president of Princeton Theological Seminary, says, "The future of the Church could be with a reformed Catholicism and a matured Pentecostalism" (66:40). Dr. Henry Pitney Van Dusen of Union Theological Seminary, says:

> The presence of the charismatic (pentecostal) move-ment among us is said to make a new era in the development of Christianity. This new Pentecost will appear to future historians as a "true reformation" (compared to that of the 16th century) from which will spring a third force in the Christian world (Protestant-Catholic-Pentecostal) (64:28).

Is it any wonder that Cardinal Leon Josef Suenens, primate of Belgium and the one charged with the over-sight of the worldwide charismatic renewal within the Roman Catholic Church, would address a clergy gather-ing in Oklahoma City using these words:

> Young men have visions and old men have dreams. And since I will be 75 very soon, one of my dreams is to seek the visible unity of the church coming in the not-too-distant future (76:42).

Later he addressed an evening "Jesus 79" rally in Myriad Arena and, stating that the church had been torn by disunity for four centuries, he expressed a prayerful hope that the day for visible Christian unity will rapidly dawn. He continued:

> We must close forever and ever the past, said the Cardinal, referring to the previous four centuries of "bitterness, war, and hatred" among churchmen. Let us look at each other with the eyes of Jesus Christ and say, "I love you," he added to sustained cheers (76:42).

It is certainly clear that leaders and many followers in both Protestant and Roman Catholic quarters expect the present ecumenism to lead eventually to union!

Such a move would have been unthinkable to most Protestants twenty years ago. Many today would still feel that this would be out of the question. Yet who would have believed twenty years ago that today we would be witnessing the gathering of Protestant and Roman Catholic charismatics joining hands idyllicly and singing, "We are one in the Spirit?"

The answer to that question might be surprising to most Protestants. In 1964 Roman Catholic writer Louis Bouyer made these stunning observations when writing concerning the charismatic roots:

> We see in every Protestant country, Christians who owed their religion to the movement we have called, in general, Revivalism, attain a more or less complete rediscovery of Catholicism (4:186).

> ... the instinctive orientation of the revivals toward the Catholic ... would bring in that way a reconciliation between the Protestant movement and the Church ... (4:197)

In commenting on this book, the editor of *Present Truth* says:

> Bouyer closes with an appeal to his fellow Catholics to prepare for the inevitable return of the "separated brethren" under the influence of contemporary revivals (64:26).

Can it be that the Catholic "spider" is about to welcome the charismatic "fly" into its parlor? The astounding changes in the religious world, produced by those misled about Biblical unity, would make it seem very possible.

CONCLUSION

It needs to be emphasized in conclusion that, though our position is contrary to that of the charismatics, we are desirous of everything God has for us. If the transient gift of tongues was for today, we would be the first to seek the blessing. We want—all of us—everything that God has for us for this present age!

However, we refuse to allow the subjectivity of our feelings to be a substitute for the teaching of the Scriptures on these matters. God's truth is objectively laid down in the Bible and, as has been reiterated throughout this treatment of the subject, what we seek and receive must be founded upon and bounded by the Word of God. We cannot dictate to God what He must do, or state to others what He will do, apart from what He has eternally written in His inerrant and unchangeable Scriptures.

In 1 Cor. 14:37 Paul ends up his three chapters of teaching on the gifts of the Holy Spirit with these words, "If any man think himself to be a prophet, or spiritual, let him acknowledge that the things that I write unto you are the commandments of the Lord." The word "acknowledge" is *epignōsketo*, from a combination *ginōskō* meaning "to know," and the intensive *epi* meaning "thoroughly" (47:27). We are to know thoroughly, to recognize completely, that apart from "the commandments of the Lord" there is no spirituality, neither any basis for the practice of the gift of tongues.

John MacArthur is clear on this matter when he states that Paul claims:

> ... that the truly spiritual ones were not those who were carried or led away. They used to be carried away into ecstatic orgiastic kinds of activities, but that wasn't supposed to be true anymore. The truly

spiritual person is not swept away into trances, ecstasies, and emotional frenzies. When a person is out of control, it is never a Christian use of any gift of the Spirit. Somebody may say that he has been slain in the Spirit; he may have been "slain," but it has not been in the Spirit (24:115).

What we need is not a step backward to the temple worship of Corinth but a sure interpretation of the Word of God as the final authority in all matters of faith and practice.

You see, people who are "spiritual" are people who walk so as to please God. But to please God a person must objectively control his life according to His Word. If one subjectively establishes his faith and practice, then he lives as those who are ignorant of God's inspired directives in the Bible. Such people are, in turn, to be ignored by others as being false in doctrine and manner of life. Thus, Paul literally writes in 1 Cor. 14:38, "But if anyone is ignorant (of this), he is ignored." (16:916) That is, the person who ignores God's Word in order to build his own spiritual knowledge and custom (his personal Bible) is to be ignored in kind by others.

While we want every blessing and gift God has for us, we *must be absolutely sure* that what we seek after is the objective promise of the Scriptures for our lives in this present age. Using any other authority, including subjective authority, we would not be spiritual or well-pleasing in God's sight. Therefore, far from being unspiritual to reject the charismatic claims concerning what the Bible teaches is a transient gift, it is an absolute spiritual necessity for us so to do.

As true today as when Joshua received the promise, are the words:

> This book of the law shall not depart out of thy mouth; but thou shalt meditate therein day and night, that thou mayest observe to do according to all that is written therein: for then thou shalt make thy way prosperous, and then thou shalt have good success (Josh. 1:8).

May God give us wisdom to make this our practice of life, in a generation misled about the gift of tongues.

BIBLIOGRAPHY

BOOKS

1. Bagster, Samuel and Sons, *The Analytical Greek Lexicon.* London: Samuel Bagster and Sons, n.d.
2. Basham, Don W., *Ministering the Baptism in the Holy Spirit.* Springdale, Pa.: Whitaker House, 1971.
3. Bergsma, Stuart, *Speaking with Tongues.* Grand Rapids, Mich.: Baker Book House, 1965.
4. Bouyer, Louis, *The Spirit and Forms of Protestantism.* Cleveland, Ohio: World Publishing Co., 1964.
5. Bruce, F. F., *The Spreading Flame.* Grand Rapids, Mich.: Wm. B. Eerdmans Publishing Co., 1958.
6. Bruner, Frederick Dale, *A Theology of the Holy Spirit.* Grand Rapids, Mich.: Wm. B. Eerdmans Publishing Co., 1970.
7. Bryant, James W., *The Doctrine of the Holy Spirit in the New Testament.* Dallas, Tex.: Crescendo Book Publications, 1973, Vol. 2, No. 2.
8. Burdick, Donald W., *Tongues: To Speak or Not to Speak.* Chicago: Moody Press, 1973.
9. Clemens, David A., *Steps to Maturity.* Upper Darby, Pa.: Bible Club Movement, 1975, Vol. 1.
10. Criswell, W. A., *The Holy Spirit in Today's World.* Grand Rapids, Mich.: Zondervan Publishing House, 1967.
11. Cutten, George B., *Speaking with Tongues Historically and Psychologically Considered.* New Haven, Conn.: Yale University, 1927.
12. Dillow, Joseph, *Speaking in Tongues: Seven Crucial Questions.* Grand Rapids, Mich.: Zondervan Publishing House, 1976.
13. *Encylopaedia Britannica.* Chicago/London/Toronto/Geneva/Sydney/Tokyo/Manila/Seoul/Johannesburg: William Benton, Publisher, 1968 Edition, Vol. 22.
14. Farrar, Frederic W., *The Early Days of Christianity.* 2 Volumes, London, Paris & New York: Cassell, Petter, Galpin & Co., 1882, Vol. 2.

15. Fife, Eric S., *The Holy Spirit.* Grand Rapids, Mich.: Zondervan Publishing House, 1978.
16. Findlay, G. G., "St. Paul's First Epistle to the Corinthians." *The Expositor's Greek Testament.* 5 Vols. Grand Rapids, Mich.: Wm. B. Eerdmans Publishing Co., 1956, Vol. 2.
17. Gardiner, George E., *The Corinthian Catastrophe.* Grand Rapids, Mich.: Kregel Publications, 1975.
18. Gee, Donald, *Now That You've Been Baptized in the Spirit.* Springfield, Mo.: Gospel Publishing House, 1972.
19. Gordon, A.J., *The Ministry of the Spirit.* Philadelphia: The Judson Press, 1949.
20. Kelsey, Morton T., *Tongue Speaking: An Experiment in Spiritual Experience.* Garden City, N.Y.: Doubleday, 1964.
21. Kittel, Gerherd, *Theological Dictionary of the New Testament.* 9 Vols. Grand Rapids, Mich.: Wm. B. Eerdmans Publishing Co., 1967, Vol. 1.
22. Knowling, R. J., "The Acts of the Apostles." *The Expositor's Greek Testament.* 5 Vols. Grand Rapids, Mich.: Wm. B. Eerdmans Publishing Co., 1956, Vol. 2.
23. Luce, Alice F., *Pictures of Pentecost.* Springfield, Mo.: Gospel Publishing House, 1950.
24. MacArthur, John F., Jr., *The Charismatics.* Grand Rapids, Mich.: Zondervan Publishing House, 1979.
25. Martin, Ira Jay, *Glossolalia in the Apostolic Church.* Berea, Ky.: Berea College, 1960.
26. Matteson, Earle E., "Should All Speak with Tongues?" *The Biblical Faith of Baptists.* Toronto, Canada: The Bryant Press, 1968, Book 3.
27. Matthews, Victor, *Growth in Grace.* Grand Rapids, Mich.: Zondervan Publishing House, 1970.
28. Morris, Henry M., *The Bible Has the Answer.* Nutley, N.J.: The Craig Press, 1971.
29. Moule, H. C. G., *Person and Work of the Holy Spirit.* Grand Rapids, Mich.: Kregel Publications, 1977.
30. O'Connor, Edward, *Pentecost in the Catholic Church.* Pecos, N. M.: Dover Publications, 1970.
31. _____, *The Pentecostal Movement in the Catholic Church.* Notre Dame, Ind.: Ave Maria Press, 1971.
32. Roberts, Oral, *The Baptism with the Holy Spirit.* Tulsa, Okla. Oral Roberts, 1966.
33. Robertson, A. T., *Word Pictures in the New Testament.* 6 Vols. Nashville, Tenn. Broadman Press, 1931, Vol. 4.

34. Robertson and Plummer, "1 Corinthians." *The International Critical Commentary.* Edinburgh: T & T Clark, 1914.

35. Ryrie, Charles Caldwell, *Balancing the Christian Life.* Chicago, Ill.: Moody Press, 1969.

36. _____, *The Holy Spirit.* Chicago: Moody Press, 1979.

37. Samarin, William J., *Tongues of Men and Angels.* New York: Macmillan Co., 1972.

38. Schofield, A. T., *Christian Sanity.* London, England: Marshall Brothers, n.d.

39. Shaw, George, *The Spirit in Redemption.* New York, N.Y.: Christian Alliance Publishing Co., 1910.

40. Sherrill, John L., *They Speak with Other Tongues.* Old Tappan, N.J.: Fleming H. Revell Co., 1965.

41. Strauss, Lehman, *The Third Person.* Neptune, N.J.: Loizeaux Brothers, 1954.

42. Sweeting, William J., *The Power for Christian Living.* (Adult Teacher), Denver, Colo.: Baptist Publications, 1962.

43. Thayer, J. H., *Greek-English Lexicon of the New Testament.* New York: American Book, 1889.

44. Torrey, R. A., *What the Bible Teaches.* Old Tappan, N.J.: Fleming H. Revell Co., 1933.

45. _____, *Why God Used D. L. Moody.* Old Tappan, N.J.: Fleming H. Revell Co., 1923.

46. Unger, Merrill F., *The Baptism & Gifts of the Holy Spirit.* Chicago: Moody Press, 1978.

47. Vine, W. E., *An Expository Dictionary of New Testament Words.* 4 Vols. in 1. Old Tappan, N.J.: Fleming H. Revell Co., 1966, Vol. 1.

48. _____, *An Expository Dictionary of New Testament Words.* 4 Vols. in 1. Old Tappan, N.J.: Fleming H. Revell Co., 1966, Vol. 2.

49. _____, *An Expository Dictionary of New Testament Words.* 4 Vols. in 1. Old Tappan, N.J.: Fleming H. Revell Co., 1966, Vol. 3.

50. _____, *An Expository Dictionary of New Testament Words.* 4 Vols. in 1. Old Tappan, N.J.: Fleming H. Revell Co., 1966, Vol. 4.

51. Walvoord, John F., *The Holy Spirit.* Grand Rapids, Mich.: Zondervan Publishing House, 1978.

52. Witty, Robert G., *Holy Spirit Power.* Jacksonville, Fla.: Pioneer Press, 1966.

BOOKLETS

53. Clark, Stephen B., *Baptized in the Spirit.* Pecos, N.M.: Dove Publications, 1970.
54. Hall, Donald E., *Cure for Charismatics.* Leader's resource Guide. Denver, Colo.: Published by Accent Books a Division of B/P Publications, 1975.
55. Hitt, Russell T., *The New Pentecostalism.* Reprinted Eternity magazine. Philadelphia, Pa.: n.d.
56. Keiper, Ralph L., *Tongues and the Holy Spirit.* Chicago: Moody Press, 1963.
57. Lightner, Robert P., *Speaking in Tongues.* Des Plaines, Ill.: Regular Baptist Press, 1965.
58. Scroggie, W. Graham, *Speaking with Tongues What Saith the Scriptures?* New York: The Book Stall,1919.
59. Solbrekken, Emil, *The Wonderful Spirit of God.* White Rock, BC., Canada: Solbrekken Evangelistic Association, 1969.
60. Sugden, Howard F., *The Signs of an Apostle.* Lansing, Mich.: South Baptist Church, 1973.
61. Van Gorder, Paul R., *Charismatic Confusion.* Grand Rapids, Mich. Radio Bible Class, 1972.

PERIODICALS

62. Benn, Gerry, "Biblical Reasons Why I Am Not a Charismatic." *Truth Aflame.* London Baptist Seminary, Aug. 1979.
63. Boyd, J. R., "The Holy Spirit and Tongues." *The Berean Ambassador.* Sept. 1976.
64. Brinsmead, Robert D., "Protestant Revivalism, Pentecostalism and the Drift Back to Rome." *Present Truth.* Special Issue 1972.
65. _____, "The Current Religious Scene and the Gospel," *Present Truth.* Feb. 1974.
66. Chandler, Russell, "Fanning the Charismatic Fire." *Christianity Today.* Nov. 24, 1967.
67. Fiske, Edward B., "Look Who's Speaking in Tongues Now." *Christian Herald.* Sept. 1974.
68. Gundry, Robert H., "Ecstatic Utterance (N.E.B.)?" *Journal of Theological Studies.* Vol. 17, 1966.
69. Gurr, Eric T., "The Gift of Tongues." *The Gospel Witness.* Mar. 31, 1977.
70. Hodges, Zane C., A Symposim on the Tongues Movement —"The Purpose of Tongues." *Bibliotheca Sacra.* July-Sept. 1963.

71. Johnson, S. Lewis, Jr., A Symposium on the Tongues Movement—"The Gift of Tongues and the Book of Acts." *Bibliotheca Sacra.* Oct.-Dec. 1963.
72. McClelland, James, "Protest." *The Revivalist.* Feb. 1977.
73. Pattison, E. Mansell, "Speaking in Tongues and about Tongues." *Christian Standard.* Feb. 15, 1964.
74. Paxton, Geoffrey J., "The Current Religious Scene and the Bible." *Present Truth.* Feb. 1974.
75. Pickford, J. H., "Baptists and the Charismatic Movement." *Evangelical Baptist.* Dec. 1969.
76. Plowman, Edward E. & Wagner, John, "Jesus 79: Pentecost Rallies Spread a Grassroots Unity." *Christianity Today.* June 29, 1979.
77. Rogers, Cleon L., "The Gift of Tongues in the Post Apostolic Church." *Bibliotheca Sacra.* Apr.-June 1965.
78. Welmers, William E., Article in *Christianity Today.* Nov. 8, 1963.
79. Wilson, Robert W., "Tongues and the Baptism of the Holy Spirit." *Evangelical Baptist.* May 1964.
80. Unknown, "Spiritual Discernment — Are Tongues Divine or Devilish?" *The Alliance Witness.* Mar. 2, 1966.

UNPUBLISHED MATERIALS

81. Brown, William Gordon, "Pentecostalism — an Examination of its History and its Distinctives." A thesis presented to the Faculty of the Winona Lake School of Theology, July 1961.
82. Wolfram, Walter A., "The Sociolinguistes of Glossolalia." Unpublished Master's thesis, Hartford Seminary Foundation, Hartford, Conn., 1966. (Quoted by Donald W. Burdick in *Tongues: To Speak or Not to Speak).*

BIBLE TRANSLATIONS

83. Williams, Charles B., *The New Testament in the Language of the People.* Chicago: Moody Press, 1958.